This Old House
fun family
projects

Projects by Edward Potokar
Photographs by Wendell T. Webber
Illustrations by Carl Wiens
Edited by Hylah Hill and Mark Powers

fun family
projects →

STILTS p. 36

BIRD FEEDER p. 44

SANDBOX p. 54

TOY CHEST p. 90

SOCCER GOAL p. 98

RAISED GARDEN p. 106

TOOLBOX — p. 12

FORT — p. 20

STEP STOOL — p. 28

EASEL — p. 64

LEMONADE STAND — p. 74

MINI-GOLF COURSE — p. 82

WALL CUBBIES — p. 116

BAT HOUSE — p. 124

TREE SWING — p. 134

3

Tools are cool.

When you were a kid, was there anything more fascinating than Mom or Dad's toolbox? For both of us, it was a treasure trove of oddities—weird-shaped pliers, screwdrivers with different heads, rough-to-the-touch files, and fasteners of all shapes and sizes. Of course, the king of the toolbox was the hammer. *Every* kid knows what to use that for: Pounding any available surface.

It's an innate pleasure that kids can't get enough of—just ask your dented floor.

But here's an idea: Save the floor and harness that natural energy, enthusiasm, and drive for good by building something with your hammer-happy little ones that they can enjoy for years to come.

Inside you'll find 15 kid-friendly projects, all developed and tested by the crew at *This Old House*. That's 15 chances to spend a day with the kids and help them master valuable skills while you all learn how to build a simple sandbox, make a bird feeder, or construct a soccer goal.

Each project has a bonus page, too. Want to serve strawberry lemonade at your colorful stand? You'll find the recipe. Want to know which seeds will attract which birds to your feeder or how to make a flag for your backyard fort? You'll find those answers.

These projects will be great fun for the whole family, but we can't forget about being careful. Throughout the book there are special tips on proper tool handling and shop safety for kids.

Now what are you waiting for? Grab some tools and supplies, clear some space in the shop, and start hammering!

Hylah and Mark

safety first

12 SIMPLE RULES FOR YOU AND YOUR FAMILY TO FOLLOW IN THE WORKSHOP

1> Show how to carry tools the right way.

Like scissors, tools should be carried with bits or blades pointing down and away from the body. Teach children to put tools down some-place safe when they are not in use and never to run in the workshop with a tool in hand.

2> Hey, kids: Be sure to dress right.

Roll up long sleeves and tuck in shirttails that might get in your way. Also, button up shirtfronts so that clothing doesn't get caught on a tool. If you have long hair, tie it back so that you can see. And don't forget about your feet: Wear protective closed-toe shoes or boots when working in the shop.

3> Keep dangerous tools off-limits.

Other than lightweight screwguns and sanders, most power tools are too heavy and dangerous for young kids to use by themselves. Putting locks on power plugs prevents them from being used when you're not around. Keep sharp-edged hand tools, like utility knives and chisels, locked up in a box or chest.

4> Hey, kids: Stay focused.

Pets, iPods, and siblings draw attention away from the task at hand and increase the chance of a mishap. Stow your toys and gadgets, and say good-bye to Fido for the afternoon. A messy shop is also a distraction—and a hazard if tools can be knocked off benches or walls. Help Mom and Dad keep the shop neat.

5> Use softwoods.

Dense woods, such as oak, maple, and ash, can be tough for kids to cut, drill, sand, and shape by themselves. They'll have an easier time working with pine and cedar, to name a few.

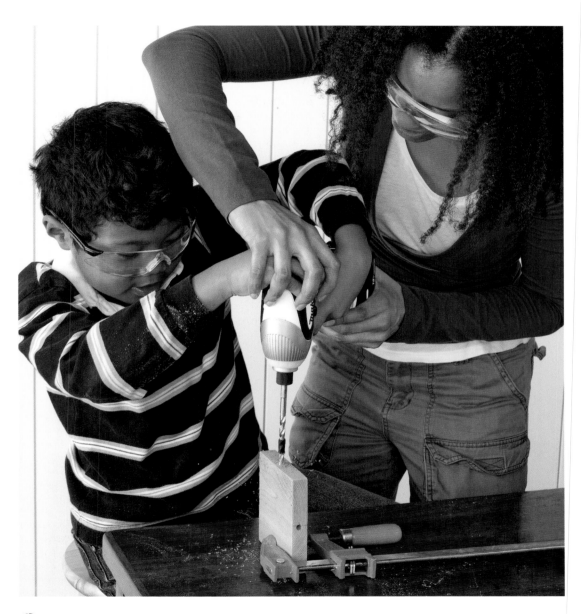

6> Supervise tool use.

Until you're sure children have good control over a tool and know the correct safety routines, keep an eye on them whenever a tool is being used. In case of an accident, keep a fully stocked first-aid kit in the shop. (You might need it for yourself as well.)

Use a tennis ball to save your kid's noggin!

A ThumbSaver will protect your fingers!

8> **Clamp your work.**
Holding both the workpiece and a tool is too hard for small hands. Steady the workpiece with a vise or clamps so that both hands can be on the tool. (This also keeps saw teeth away from fingers.)

9> **Start with a small handsaw.**
If you allow your child to use a handsaw, make sure it's short, sharp, and fine-toothed. Japanese pull-type saws with more than 12 teeth per inch are easier to start and less likely to snag. Caution children to always work with two hands on the saw's handle—which provides better control and keeps fingers away from the blade—and make sure it's big enough for a doubled-up grip.

7> **Cushion hammer blows.**
Hammering nails is something kids seem to enjoy. A child will have better control of a lightweight hammer (10 ounces or less) than a small "kid's hammer." A magnetic nail holder like the ThumbSaver keeps fingers safe from misplaced blows, and a tennis ball stuck on the claw end of the hammer prevents painful collisions with a child's head on the backswing.

10> **Lower the worktable.**
Kids need a working surface positioned at a comfortable height so that they have better control of their tools and can easily see what they're doing.

11> Hey, kids: Protect those eyes!

Like seatbelts in a car, eye protection should be mandatory for anyone picking up a power tool. Be sure to wear safety glasses when you and your parents are drilling, cutting, or sanding. Make sure Mom and Dad have them on too!

12> Keep cleanup in mind.

Choose water-based paints, stains, and glues. They're a lot easier to clean up than solvent-based materials (as long as you wash them off before they dry). And they're safer, too.

Most important: Keep your pencil and your mind sharp.

Look for safety tips throughout the projects' instructions. And be sure to measure twice and cut once.

NOTE TO READERS: Almost any do-it-yourself project involves risk of some sort. Your tools, materials, and skills will vary, as will conditions on your project site. This Old House and the editors of this book have made every effort to be complete and accurate in the instructions. We will, however, assume no responsibility or liability for injuries, damages, or losses incurred in the course of the family projects. Always follow the manufacturer's operating instructions in the use of tools, check and follow your local building codes, and observe all safety precautions. Children should be supervised by an adult at all times while working on the projects and playing on or with the finished projects.

{ HOW TO USE THIS BOOK }

Each chapter starts with a handy guide that tells you the rough cost of the project, the approximate time it will take, and what to expect along the way.

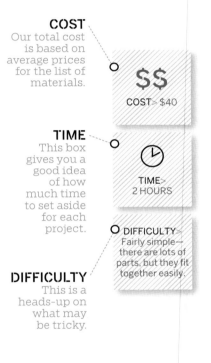

COST
Our total cost is based on average prices for the list of materials.

$$
COST> $40

TIME
This box gives you a good idea of how much time to set aside for each project.

TIME> 2 HOURS

DIFFICULTY> Fairly simple—there are lots of parts, but they fit together easily.

DIFFICULTY
This is a heads-up on what may be tricky.

THISOLDHOUSE.COM/BOOKS

This companion website for *Fun Family Projects* has templates and step-by-step videos for all the projects.

 This symbol indicates an online template.

 This symbol indicates an online video.

glossary +tips

PEARLS OF WORKSHOP
WISDOM FROM THE CREW
OF THIS OLD HOUSE

Bar clamp: Used to hold together wide pieces, like the sides of a box. The screw-down grip allows you to increase the clamp pressure when a strong hold is needed. This clamp comes in different lengths.

Combination square: An adjustable square that helps you measure, trace cutlines, and check the right-angle accuracy of corners. Hold its head against the edge of a board to trace perpendicular or 45-degree cutlines. Adjust the length of the ruler to measure or mark the depth of a cut. You can also use the edge of the ruler as a guide (or fence) for your power saw to ride along.

Drill/driver: A versatile power tool that can bore holes or drive screws, depending on the type of bit you use. **Countersink bits** bore a shallow hole that lets the screwhead rest below the surface. **Spade bits** have a wide cutting end for quickly drilling large holes. **Hole saws** are circular, serrated bit attachments for drilling large, clean holes in sheet goods.

TIPS > *Use a slow speed for torque (working power) to drive screws.*
> *Set it on the highest speed when boring holes, and move the bit in and out as you drill to clear out the wood dust from your hole.*
> *Before sinking a fastener, you'll probably need to drill a pilot hole. Pilot holes create an accurate path for the screw and prevent the fastener from splitting the material. They also make it easier to screw through thick or hardwood material. To find the correct size drill bit for your pilot hole, hold the bit against the shank of the screw you are sinking. You've chosen the correct size when you can barely see the sides of the fastener past the bit.*

Framing square: A fixed, L-shaped tool that consists of a long ruler called the blade and a shorter ruler called the tongue. Use it to check the right-angle accuracy of corners in larger lumber-frame projects. It also makes a great straightedge for laying out pencil lines and a guide for safe, straight cutting with a utility knife.

Hammer: An 8- to 13-ounce finish hammer is perfect for most projects in this book. **TIPS** > *Don't choke up on the handle. Hold it near the end for the best control and most hitting power.*
> *Remember to keep your eyes on the nailhead as you swing, and you'll never miss your target.*
> *A sharply curved claw offers better leverage for pulling out mistakes.*

Jigsaw: An easy-to-use, relatively quiet power saw that can cut intricate curves and circles.
TIPS > *Use higher speeds for long, straight cuts in thicker material, and slower speeds for thinner material and short or complex cuts.*
> *Be sure to use the correct blade for the material you are cutting. For thicker lumber, use a blade with 5 to 6 teeth per inch (tpi). A blade with 10 to 12 tpi will cut thinner woods and plywood more cleanly.*
> *Allow the saw to reach its operating speed before the blade touches the wood, and always let the saw come to a complete stop before removing it from the material.*
> *Always make sure the board or panel*

you are cutting is fully supported and clamped so that it won't cave in on your saw after it has been cut.
> *Sawing is best left to an adult, but kids can help by catching the pieces as they fall. Just make sure they're standing far from the saw—and don't let them lift up on the wood as it's cut, because that can pinch the blade.*

Paintbrush: For the latex paints and stains recommended in these projects, use a bristle brush made of nylon or polyester. It holds its shape better.
TIPS > *Load only the tips of the bristles—about one-third of the brush. Be sure to clean and comb out your brush at the end of the day.*

Random-orbit sander: An easy-to-use oscillating sanding tool that lets you sand without having to strictly follow the grain of the wood.
TIPS > *Let the sander do the work by using light downward pressure as you hold it. Keep the pad completely flat to avoid divots.*
> *When choosing paper for your sander, remember: The higher the grit number, the finer the sanding.*

Spring clamps: Like an extra set of hands, they offer an instant, light grip on your workpiece.

build a toolbox

$$
COST> $40

TIME>
2 HOURS

DIFFICULTY>
Fairly simple—
there are lots of
parts, but they
fit together
easily.

IF YOUR LITTLE BUILDERS inherited the DIY gene, then they're more or less programmed to dive into Mom and Dad's tools. So maybe you should think about giving the handy helpers their own set—the better to get them involved while keeping your precious collection from getting trashed.

This toolbox is just the thing to hold smaller, basic items that fit a young do-it-yourselfer's hands, including a hammer, saws, pliers, and screwdrivers. Building it is easy: The tools required are probably already in your stash, and the materials are readily available at a home center and a sporting goods store. Set yourself up on a sturdy worktable—in the workshop, the garage, even the playroom. The fun is in having something for everyone to do and getting in good practice for future projects.

TOOLS YOU'LL NEED>

- Tape measure
- Hammer and nailset
- Combination square
- Spring clamps
- Jigsaw, circular saw, or handsaw
- Straightedge saw guide
- Safety glasses
- Drill/driver with ⅜-inch drill bit and ½- and 1-inch spade bits
- Random-orbit sander or sanding block
- Bar clamps
- Putty knife
- 2-inch paintbrush

MATERIALS TO BUY>

- 2×4-foot piece of ½-inch birch veneer plywood
- Plastic jars (optional: for keeping nails and screws organized in the box)
- 120-grit sandpaper
- Stainable wood glue
- Clean rag
- 4d finish nails
- Stainable wood putty
- Water-based stain
- Latex gloves
- Hockey-stick tape
- Nail-on furniture glides (optional)

{ HOW IT GOES TOGETHER }

There are seven parts to this toolbox, and they will all fit on one 2-by-4-foot sheet of plywood. If you line up parts adjacent to one another so that they have a common cutline, make sure you account for the ⅛-inch kerf that will be eaten up by the saw blade with each cut.

Birch veneer plywood is the best choice as a material for this project because it's strong, has a smooth face, and takes stains or paints well. Construction plywood will also work, but the face will not be as smooth.

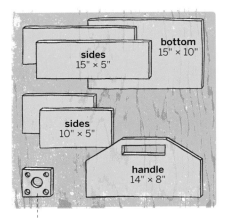

bottom
15" × 10"

sides
15" × 5"

sides
10" × 5"

handle
14" × 8"

tool holder
4¼" × 4¼"

ONLINE: Download the handy full-size template at thisoldhouse.com/books

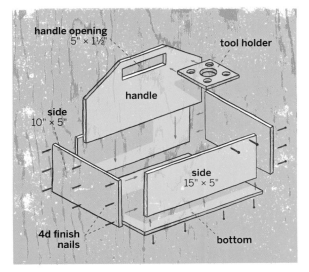

handle opening
5" × 1½"

tool holder

handle

side
10" × 5"

side
15" × 5"

4d finish nails

bottom

STEP_1 Cut out the parts

> Using spring or bar clamps, clamp the plywood to a sturdy worktable. Make sure the piece you will cut hangs free over the edge.
> Using a jigsaw, circular saw, or handsaw, cut the plywood into the individual pieces. For added accuracy, clamp a straightedge saw guide next to your saw.

TO PARENTS:
Using a jigsaw or circular saw is a job for grown-ups. Be sure you and your children wear safety glasses before you start.

STEP_2 Lay out the handle grip

> Using a combination square, lay out a 5-by-1½-inch rectangle near the top of the handle to denote where the grip will go. Make sure that it is centered. To create the angled sides of the handle, mark the top of the handle 1½ inches from either side of the grip; mark each side of the handle 5 inches from the bottom. Draw a diagonal line between these marks on each side of the grip.
> Clamp the handle piece to the table. Using a drill/driver fitted with a ⅜-inch bit, cut holes in the four corners of the rectangle. Make sure to stay inside the lines. These holes will allow you to insert and turn the jigsaw blade to make a cutout.

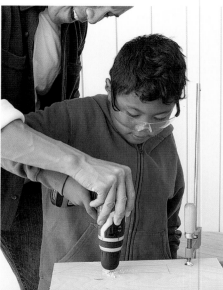

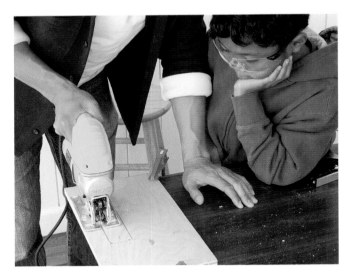

STEP_3
Cut the handle grip

> Set the jigsaw flat on the workpiece, with the blade in one of the holes.
> Slowly cut along one layout line until you reach the next corner. Stop the saw, turn it to face the next line, then start cutting again. Continue in this manner from corner to corner until the center portion is removed from the handle.
> Using the jigsaw, cut off each angled side.

The holes in the tool holder are set along an X formation.

STEP_4
Drill the tool holder

> Clamp the tool holder insert on top of some scrap wood. Using ½- and 1-inch spade bits, drill holes in an X formation on the square.

HEY, KIDS!
You can help with the sanding. Just make sure a parent is there to watch you because the sander moves a lot when it vibrates.

STEP_5
Sand each piece

> Using a random-orbit sander and 120-grit sandpaper, sand all the toolbox parts until they're smooth and free of splinters. (Make sure the dust bag is on the back of the sander.) Smooth the edges of the plywood as well, but be careful not to round them over.

STEP_ 6
Glue and assemble the pieces

> Put a thin bead of stainable wood glue on the short ends of the long side pieces. Lay the small sides over these ends. Using bar clamps, hold the box together. Wipe up any glue that squeezes out with a damp rag.

HEY, KIDS! You can help by applying the glue to the ends of the wood while your parents clamp the pieces.

TO PARENTS: Setting nails is tricky. Have your kids practice on scrap wood first, or do this step yourself. Kids can still help out by filling the nail holes with putty and sanding it when it's dry.

STEP_ 7
Nail the box together

> Hammer 4d finish nails at the corners, through the ends of the small sides, and into the long sides. Do this for all four corners, using four nails along each side.
> Remove the clamps. Run a bead of glue along the bottom edges, and lay the bottom piece over the sides. Clamp the bottom piece on, then nail it in place with 4d finish nails.
> Glue and nail the tool holder insert to the side of the handle. Put glue on the side edges of the handle and on the outer corner of the tool holder, and place the whole assembly in the toolbox. Clamp, then nail it in place.
> Using a nailset, sink all the nails below the surface. Fill the holes with stainable wood putty. Let it dry, then sand it smooth.

STEP_ **8** Apply the stain

> Wearing latex gloves and using a 2-inch paintbrush, brush stain onto the wood, then wipe it off with a clean rag. (The more you leave on, the darker it will get.) Let it dry.

HEY, KIDS!
Why not choose your favorite color for your toolbox?

STEP_ **9** Put on the finishing touches

> Cut a few lengths of hockey-stick tape, and use them to wrap the handle to make a comfortable grip.
> If you want, nail furniture glides onto the box's bottom to keep it from scratching floors. Then fill it with tools, grab it by the handle, and you're ready to go!

ONLINE VIDEO: Watch the step-by-step video at thisoldhouse.com/books

PICK YOUR TOOLS

Every handy kid needs some tools, whether they're for helping with weekend fixes or building a school project. Most adult tools come in sizes small hands can hold. Fill your new toolbox with this group of basics.

square

tape measure

pencil

torpedo level

for MEASURING

small handsaw

Japanese pull saw

for CUTTING

for ATTACHING

for TIGHTENING

needle-nose pliers

Phillips-head screwdriver

adjustable wrench

lightweight hammer (10 oz. or less)

flat screwdriver

tongue-and-groove pliers

small staple gun

build a fort

A BACKYARD FORT is the perfect place to let kids' imaginations run wild. They can create a magical world of knights and dragons or pirates and buried treasure—or just a kid-run kingdom. The design of this fort encourages tons of fun, with a super-cool kid-sized hatch—complete with a peephole to check out visitors—and a flag that kids can design and make themselves. There are also two built-in seats so that little warriors—or Mom and Dad—can take a breather between make-believe battles. Set aside an afternoon to cut and assemble the parts, and you'll have a playhouse retreat for years to come.

$$$

COST> $175

TIME>
3 HOURS

DIFFICULTY>
The assembly
is basic, but
carrying fencing
requires two
adults.

TOOLS
YOU'LL NEED>
- Tape measure
- Jigsaw
- Combination square
- Handsaw
- Drill/driver with ⅜-inch and 1-inch spade bits
- Safety glasses
- Hacksaw

MATERIALS
TO BUY>
- 4-foot-high stockade fencing (four sections at least 5 feet long)
- One 8-foot 2×4
- One 8-foot 2×3
- 2-foot-square section of ½-inch pressure-treated plywood
- Eight L-brackets (4 inches by 1 inch)
- 1⅝-inch deck screws
- 3½-inch deck screws
- 5 feet of ½-inch PVC pipe
- PVC pipe cap
- Two 3½-inch door hinges
- Flag
- Wire

22

{ HOW IT GOES TOGETHER }

This fort is made from fencing sections, so most of the cutting and assembly centers around the braces that hold the fence pickets together. The most complicated part of the project is creating the hatch, which requires making new braces to hold together the pickets after they've been cut. These need to be screwed to each picket. The other parts are simple to make. Two corner seats can be cut from a single square of plywood, and the flag is simply a piece of decorated cloth attached to a length of PVC pipe, which you can slide into holes in one corner's brace pieces.

There's a lot kids can do in building this fort. While parents will need to handle most of the heavy lifting, such as carrying the fence sections to the site, kids can help out by measuring, drilling, and holding pieces in place.

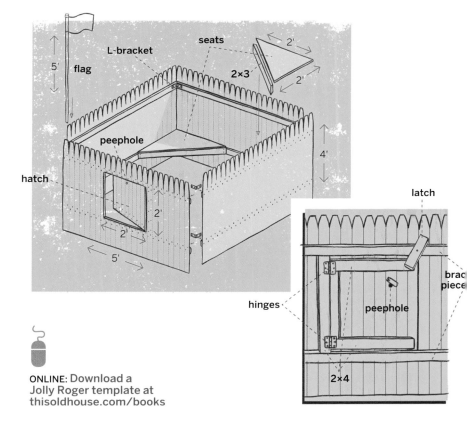

seats

5'

flag

L-bracket

2×3

2'

2'

peephole

4'

hatch

2'

2'

5'

latch

brace piece

hinges

peephole

2×4

ONLINE: Download a Jolly Roger template at thisoldhouse.com/books

STEP_1 Cut apart the fence sections

> Measure out approximately 5 feet on a section of stockade fence, and find the nearest space between two pickets. (You can approximate these measurements, as long as you create four sections that have the same number of pickets.)

> Using a jigsaw, cut through the two brace pieces on the back of the fencing at this space. Cut all four sides in this manner.

ONLINE VIDEO: Watch the step-by-step video at thisoldhouse.com/books

23

STEP_2
Miter the fence braces

> Stand the 5-foot section up. Using a combination square, mark out for a 45-degree miter cut at either end of each brace piece. (These miters will allow you to fit the fence sections together at right angles.)

> Cut these miters with a handsaw.

STEP_3 Frame out the hatch door

> Draw an outline on the front of the one fence section where you want the 2-foot-square hatch to go. Position it between the two brace pieces, with its side edges falling between pickets. Drill ⅜-inch holes to mark the door's four corners.

> Flip over the section and transfer the hatch outline to the back, using the small holes as guides.

> Measure between the brace pieces, and cut a 2×4 to that length. Position it between the braces, along the outside edge of the outline, on the side from which you want the hatch to swing. To attach the 2×4 to the back, screw through the front of the fencing with 1⅝-inch screws every 6 inches down the middle of the picket.

> Cut two more 2×4 pieces to fit inside the top and bottom edges of your hatch outline. Screw these onto the back of the fencing in the same manner. Cut a fourth 2×4 to fit between the top and bottom pieces and up against the first 2×4. You now have a frame to hold the pickets onto the hatch door.

> Attach hinges between the short and long 2×4s along the side of the hatch.

STEP_4 Cut open the hatch

> Turn the fencing over so that it's faceup. Using a jigsaw, cut open the hatch along its top and bottom edges between the corner holes. Cut all the way to the edge of the last picket attached to the hatch frame.

STEP_5 Make the peephole

> Using a drill/driver fitted with a 1-inch spade bit, drill a peephole near the top of the hatch. Attach a small scrap of wood with a single screw above the hole so that it can swing back and forth to cover the peephole.
> Make a latch from a 2×3 scrap block. Attach it to the brace above the door with a single screw so that it can swing easily to lock the hatch.

STEP_6 Set up the fort walls

> Before you bring the sides of the fort outside, brace the hatch with scrap wood screwed across the door edge; this will keep it from swinging open and hurting someone in transit.
> Carry the four fencing sections to the fort site. Lay them facedown in the area where they will stand.

STEP_7 Screw the walls together

> Bring two fencing sections together and line up the mitered corners. Using a drill/driver, screw on L-brackets to hold the corners together where the top and bottom brace pieces meet. Assemble all the corners in this way until you have a square.

STEP_8 Make the corner seats

> Using a jigsaw, cut a 2-foot-square piece of pressure-treated plywood. Cut the square in half diagonally to make two triangular seats. Using a drill/driver and 1⅝-inch screws, attach the seats to the bottom brace pieces at each back corner.

> Measure the front, diagonal edge of one seat and cut a 2×3 to this length; miter the ends with opposing 45-degree angles.

> Using a drill/driver, secure each mitered seat support to the fence braces with 3½-inch screws driven at an angle a few inches from each end.

> Screw each seat to the cross support with 1⅝-inch screws.

STEP_9 Plant the flag

> Make a flag from a piece of cloth, painting or sewing on your favorite design.

> Using a hacksaw, cut a 5-foot section of ½-inch PVC pipe. Thread thin wire through the left edge of your flag, and drop the wire at the top corner into the end of the pipe. Use a pipe cap to hold it in place. Wrap the bottom end of the wire around the pipe.

> Using a 1-inch spade bit, drill a hole through the top brace in a front corner and another hole halfway through the bottom brace directly below it. Slide the flagpole through the top hole to rest in the bottom hole. Now you're ready to man (or woman) your fort!

CREATE YOUR SHIELD

When your fort's finished, raise a flag that'll show your enemies who's in charge of your territory. You can create your own noble shield with felt glued on fabric. Here's how to get started with the design.

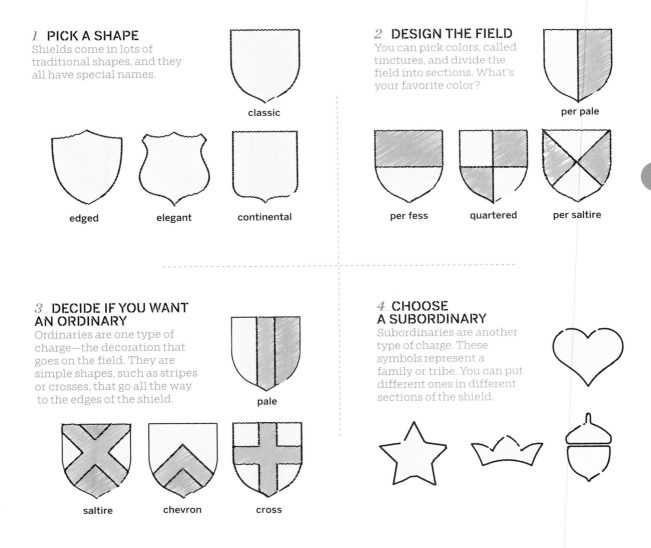

1 PICK A SHAPE
Shields come in lots of traditional shapes, and they all have special names.

classic

edged

elegant

continental

2 DESIGN THE FIELD
You can pick colors, called tinctures, and divide the field into sections. What's your favorite color?

per pale

per fess

quartered

per saltire

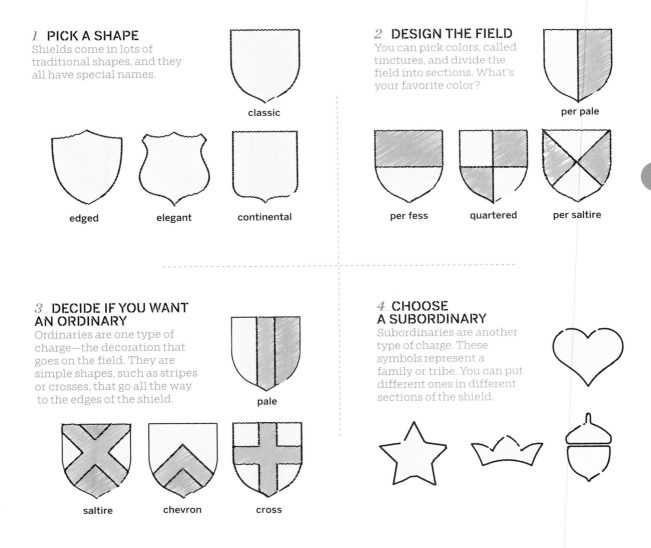

3 DECIDE IF YOU WANT AN ORDINARY
Ordinaries are one type of charge—the decoration that goes on the field. They are simple shapes, such as stripes or crosses, that go all the way to the edges of the shield.

pale

saltire

chevron

cross

4 CHOOSE A SUBORDINARY
Subordinaries are another type of charge. These symbols represent a family or tribe. You can put different ones in different sections of the shield.

build a step stool

FOR KIDS WHO live in a grown-up world, reaching things isn't always a matter of stretching their hands up—sometimes they need a boost to get to adult level. This light but very sturdy step stool is a perfect way to help little ones think big, whether they need to wash their hands, put away games and toys, or get to their favorite book. The same antiskid tape used on ladders and stairs adorns the top and makes it safe to use. Plus, its checkerboard design puts some "fun" in functional—the stool can be used for checkers or chess when work is done. Set aside just a few hours for this project and kids will have a step stool of their very own in no time flat. It's so easy (and handy to have around), you may want to make one for every room in the house.

$$
COST> $30

🕐
TIME>
3 HOURS

DIFFICULTY>
The three parts
are simple to
make and the
assembly is
straightforward.

{ HOW IT GOES TOGETHER }

The construction of this stool is very basic: Two small wood panels slot together in an X to make the legs; a square of wood is screwed onto the legs to make the top. Since it will take a lot of abuse, it's best to make the stool out of a hardwood, such as oak or maple. However, hardwoods are more difficult to cut and screw together—you'll need to drill pilot holes for your screws or you risk splitting the wood. This may be a job for a parent, because drilling into the wood without breaking the bit can be a challenge.

Children age 7 and up should be able to use a random-orbit sander with a parent's guidance. Helping with measuring, painting, drawing the squares, and sticking on the antiskid tape are also great ways for kids to get involved.

TOOLS YOU'LL NEED>

- Tape measure
- Combination square
- Bar clamps
- Safety glasses
- Jigsaw
- Drill/driver with ¼- and ³⁄₃₂-inch drill bits
- Random-orbit sander or sanding block
- Putty knife
- 2-inch paintbrush
- Framing square or ruler
- Utility scissors

MATERIALS TO BUY>

- 3-foot piece of 1×12 oak or maple
- 1⅝-inch finish screws
- 60-grit sandpaper
- 120-grit sandpaper
- Stainable wood glue
- Stainable wood putty
- Water-based stain or latex paint
- Nonskid tape
- Nail-on furniture glides

30

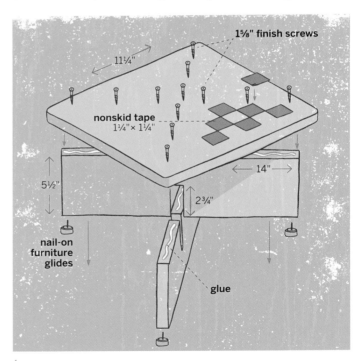

1⅝" finish screws

11¼"

nonskid tape
1¼" × 1¼"

14"

5½"

2¾"

nail-on furniture glides

glue

ONLINE: Download the handy full-size template of the crisscross legs at thisoldhouse.com/books

STEP_1
Lay out the pieces

> Using a tape measure and combination square, mark up a piece of 1×12 oak or maple (which is actually 11¼ inches wide) to make an 11¼-inch square and another piece 14 inches long.
> Draw a line to divide the second piece in half to create the two 14-inch-long crisscross legs. At the center of each of the divided pieces, mark out a rectangle that is 1 inch wide and extends halfway into each leg.

STEP_2
Cut the top and legs

> Clamp the wood to a worktable, and put on safety glasses. Using a jigsaw, cut the square top off the wood, then cut off the section with the two legs in it. Next, clamp the leg section to the table and rip it in half.

TO PARENTS: Hardwoods are difficult to cut, so work slowly and keep an eye on your cutline.

STEP_3
Make the leg slots

> Clamp one of the leg pieces to the table. Using a drill/driver fitted with a ¼-inch bit, drill two holes at the inner corners of the slot marks—these will allow you to turn the jigsaw blade. Using a jigsaw, cut the slot (be sure to stop the saw before turning the blade), keeping your blade on the inside of the line. Cut the slot on the other leg in the same manner.

32

STEP_4
Sand the pieces

> Clamp the top piece down. Using a random-orbit sander and 60-grit sandpaper, round over the corners and edges to soften them. Switch to 120-grit paper and sand all the flat surfaces on the top and legs to smooth them before painting. Make sure the dust bag is on the back of the sander.

Assemble the stool

> Lay the top piece flat on a table. Using a framing square or a ruler, lightly pencil an X from corner to opposite corner. Measure 7 inches out from the center along each line, and make a mark; because the legs are 14 inches long, they will fit between these marks when the legs are centered under the top. Using a drill/driver fitted with a 3/32-inch bit, drill pilot holes along the lines every couple of inches; make sure not to drill beyond the 7-inch marks.

> Slot the two legs together to make an X shape. You may have to hammer it down to get it tight— use a scrap of wood as a buffer between the hammer and legs.

> Place the top onto the legs and center it. Transfer the location of the pilot holes, using a small nail or a pencil lead, onto the top edge of the legs. Then remove the top, and drill pilot holes about 1¼ inches into the legs.

> Run a thin bead of wood glue along the top edge of the legs. Place the top of the stool onto the legs, and line up the pilot holes. Using a drill/driver, screw the top to the legs using 1⅝-inch finish screws. Sink them just below the surface.

> Using a putty knife, fill the screw holes with stainable putty, allow it to dry, and sand it smooth.

33

STEP_ **6** Paint the stool

> Choose your favorite color, and paint your stool with it, using latex paint and a 2-inch brush. Once the paint is dry, attach nail-on furniture glides to the four corners of the legs to keep the stool from scratching the floor.

STEP_ **7**
Lay out the squares

> Find the center point of the top again, and make a small mark. Using a ruler, measure outward in 1¼-inch increments toward the edges in all four directions. Then make lines at those marks to create a grid of eight squares by eight squares.

TO PARENTS:
This is a great step for kids to help out with, and you can even teach them about the fractions on a ruler as you mark the squares.

STEP_ **8**
Make the checkerboard

> Using a ruler and utility scissors, measure and cut out 1¼-inch squares of nonskid tape—you will need 32 total. Peel off the backing and stick the squares on. Once you finish, you're ready to play!

There are lots of different games to play on the top of your checkerboard step stool. You can play standard checkers or chess, of course. But you might want to try French checkers, where unkinged checkers can't jump other pieces. (It makes for a long but exciting game!) Or there's Giveaway checkers, in which you try to lose all your pieces to win. Here are two other games you can play.

FOX AND HOUNDS

One player must try to get his or her single checker past a row of four checkers controlled by the other player. (Even kids 5 or 6 can join the fun!) Here's how to play:

Put the hounds (four black checkers) on the black squares on a king's row and the fox (one red checker) on a black square on the opposite king's row. None of the pieces can jump, but the fox is able to move forward or backward. The hounds can only move forward.

You "win" when the fox reaches the opposite king's row or the hounds corner the fox so that he can't move.

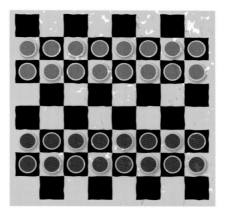

TURKISH CHECKERS

The goal is the same as in traditional checkers, but the setup and movements are different. Here's how to play:

Start with your checkers filling all the squares on the second and third rows of each side of the board. You can move and jump forward and sideways, but not diagonally. The goal is to get to the opposite king's row and capture your opponent's pieces. Once crowned, you can move forward and sideways as well as diagonally and backward.

If you capture all your opponent's pieces or they can't make any legal moves, you win.

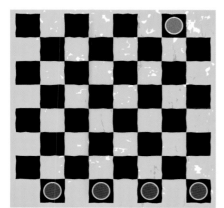

build stilts

NOT TOO LONG AGO, the folks at *This Old House* TV invited some kids into the workshop to build a few fun projects. First up: stilts!

A pair of low stilts is a great way to teach older kids about balance without sending them out on the high wire. Because stilt walking takes some skill, we recommend this project for children 8 years old and up.

Building them is quite easy, as *TOH* general contractor Tom Silva and two kid carpenters demonstrate. All it takes is a couple of pieces of lumber and some sturdy bolts, and in an hour or two you can put on your own circus show. Just be careful, and keep the clowning to a minimum.

$
COST> $50

TIME> 2 HOURS

DIFFICULTY> Learning to walk on the stilts may be harder than putting them together.

Tom Silva
TOH TV General Contractor

TOOLS YOU'LL NEED>
- Tape measure
- Straightedge
- Circular saw or jigsaw
- Hammer
- Drill/driver with #6 countersink bit and ⁵⁄₁₆-inch drill bit
- Random-orbit sander

MATERIALS TO BUY>
- 12 feet of 1½-inch-diameter pine handrail (round on one side, flat on the other)
- 3 feet of 1×8 poplar
- Wood glue
- 3d nails
- 1¼-inch deck screws
- 2-inch deck screws
- Four ¼×3½-inch carriage bolts with fender washers, lock washers, and wing nuts
- 120-grit sandpaper
- One pair of 1½-inch rubber feet (sometimes used for furniture or canes)

38

{ HOW IT GOES TOGETHER }

Stilts are simply sturdy poles with treads attached to their sides. To make the poles, Tom Silva and his handy helpers used two 6-foot lengths of pine handrail, which are flat on one side and rounded on the other. The flat side braces against the user, while the round side provides a comfortable grip.

The treads are attached to the flat sides of the poles with large supports. To make the treads and supports strong enough, Tom recommends using a hardwood, such as poplar. He used carriage bolts to attach the supports to the poles; these can be unscrewed and moved to raise or lower the height of the treads. And last, a pair of rubber feet are popped onto the bottom of the poles to keep them from slipping while you walk.

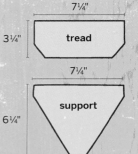

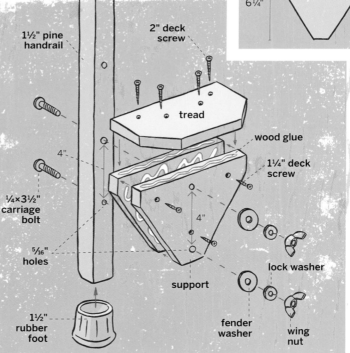

STEP_ 1 Lay out the pieces

> Using a tape measure and straightedge, lay out the treads and supports on the poplar 1×8. You will need four support pieces and two treads. Along the middle of two of the support pieces, make one mark 1 inch from the top edge and another mark exactly 4 inches from the first one. Measure carefully—later you will drill holes here for the bolts that attach the supports to the poles.

ONLINE: Download the handy full-size template of the treads and supports at thisoldhouse.com/books

STEP_ 2 Cut out the parts

> Make sure a parent does this step. Using a circular saw or jigsaw, cut out the two treads and the four support pieces from the 1×8.

STEP_ 3
Glue the supports together

> Cover the face of one support piece with wood glue, and place a second support piece on top of it. Make sure the edges line up. Then tack the two parts together by hammering 3d nails close to their center. With a damp rag, wipe up any glue that squeezes out. Repeat this with the other pair of support pieces.

STEP_ **4**

Screw the supports together

> Using a drill/driver fitted with a countersink bit, drill three pilot holes through the supports, 1 or 2 inches from each corner. Then sink 1¼-inch deck screws into these holes.

STEP_ **5** Attach the treads

> Again using a drill/driver and countersink bit, drill four pilot holes through each tread for the screws that will attach it to the support, with two holes going through the top edge of each support piece.
> Run a bead of glue along the support's long edge. Lay the tread on top of it; make sure that the long edge of the tread is aligned with the long edge of the support.
> Screw the tread to the support with 2-inch deck screws.
> Repeat this process with the other tread.

40

ONLINE VIDEO:
Watch the step-by-step video at thisoldhouse .com/books

STEP_ **6**

Drill holes for the bolts

> Using a drill/driver fitted with a ⁵⁄₁₆-inch bit, drill holes at the two marks along the middle of each support piece. These holes will hold the carriage bolts that attach the supports to the poles.

STEP_ 7 Drill holes in the poles

> Lay each pole on the work surface, flat side up. Draw a line down the middle of each pole, then mark the line in four places along the lower third of the pole. Start the marks a few inches from the bottom, and space them exactly 4 inches apart, to align with the holes in the supports.
> Hang the end of the pole over the edge of your work surface. Using a drill/driver, make a $5/16$-inch hole at each mark.

STEP_ 8 Sand the parts

> Using a random-orbit sander and 120-grit sandpaper, smooth out the treads and supports, taking down any sharp edges and corners. Hand sand the poles to be sure they have no splinters.

STEP_ 9 Assemble the stilts

> Brace the flat side of the tread assembly against the flat side of the pole, lining up the holes in the support with the two lowest holes in the pole. Thread a carriage bolt through the pole and the support at each hole. Slide a fender washer, then a lock washer, then a wing nut over the end of each bolt. Tighten the nut. You can change the height of the treads by moving them to align with higher holes.
> Fit a rubber foot over the bottom of each pole.

This Old **House**
special project

STEP_

10

Master the stilts

> To use the stilts, place the poles behind your shoulders and step onto the treads. Make sure there's an adult around the first time kids try this. With a little practice, you'll be walking tall in no time!

TOM SILVA SAYS:
"Make sure the rubber feet are on nice and tight before you take your first step."

STILT WALKING:
A brief and incomplete history

When you think of stilt walkers, what comes to mind? Perhaps those colorful circus clowns with the impossibly long legs who walk around the big top while lions jump through hoops. But did you know that stilt walking can be traced back to many historic cultures? Some, like the early Chinese, relied on stilts to get around their villages when the rivers flooded the streets. Others, like the ancient Mayans (and according to legend, the Romans, too), used stilts in religious ceremonies, maybe hoping that being higher in the sky would help the gods hear their wishes. Then there was a group of people in France who walked on stilts *all the time*.

THE STILT WALKERS OF LES LANDES

In 1891, Sylvain Dornon, a baker from southeastern France, walked on stilts from Paris to Moscow in 58 days. That's 1,830 miles! This was after walking to Paris from his home—a 435-mile warm-up.

Dornon was from Les Landes, an area known for its marshes and low vegetation. There were no roads there in the 19th century, and the region was prone to flooding, so it was much easier to get around on stilts than on foot. The Landese were agile stilt walkers, having learned the skill at an early age. Even kids walked on stilts!

The Landese were very poor people, and they raised sheep

Sylvain Dornon, on his stilts, knitting

for a living. A pair of stilts, called "tchangues," was a useful shepherding tool. On stilts, the Landese could easily navigate the marshes where the sheep grazed. And from their elevated perch, it was easy to see the flock as well as any approaching predators. The shepherds carried a staff, which helped them tend their sheep and, when fitted with a wood slat on top, acted as a stool where they would sit and knit footless stockings.

Landese stilts were 5-foot-long pieces of wood bound to the foot and leg by leather straps. Sometimes the bottom of the stilts were reinforced with a sheep's bone. The Landese mounted their stilts from a seated position on a windowsill or even a chimney mantel.

STILT WALKING AS ENTERTAINMENT

Empress Josephine of France became a fan of the Landese stilt walkers on a journey to join her husband, Emperor Napoleon Bonaparte in Bayonne. Along the way, her entourage was greeted by a group of young stilters. Their strides were so long that they easily kept up with her fast carriages. These skillful walkers stayed on to entertain

Empress Josephine

Josephine and the ladies of her court with races. When the ladies were feeling particularly devilish, they threw coins on the ground and watched the men scramble and stoop to pick up the money.

build a bird feeder

IF YOU WANT hours of quiet entertainment, build yourself a bird feeder, fill it with seeds, then watch the feathery fliers swarm. Hang it outside your kitchen or living room window, and enjoy your chirping friends all year long. Especially as the cold months approach, your backyard visitors will be happy to have the free buffet. It's a great way to learn about birds too. A field guide of your region's avian species will help you figure out who's coming to lunch (try *The Sibley Guide to Birds*). Before you know it, you'll be putting names to the faces of your new friends.

$$
COST> $35

TIME>
2 HOURS

DIFFICULTY>
The parts are
a cinch to make
and assemble.

TOOLS YOU'LL NEED>

- Tape measure
- Combination square
- Compass
- Bar clamps
- Jigsaw
- Safety glasses
- Random-orbit sander or sanding block
- Hammer
- Drill/driver with ¼-inch bit and ½-inch spade bit
- Scissors
- Wire cutters
- Screwdriver

MATERIALS TO BUY>

- 2 feet of 1×6 cedar
- 2 feet of ¼-inch dowel
- 120-grit sandpaper
- Wood glue
- 4d finish nails
- ⅜-inch rubber grommet
- Epoxy
- Copper-topped post cap for a 4×4
- 1-liter soda bottle
- Three feet of ⁵⁄₃₂-inch vinyl-covered wire
- ⅝-inch blued tacks
- Eye screw

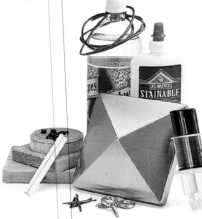

{ HOW IT GOES TOGETHER }

The bird feeder shown here looks store-bought but was made with materials from the home center and grocery store. The copper top is a cap for a 4×4 deck post, and the clear body is made from a plastic soda bottle. The rest of the feeder was cut from a single cedar board, and it all comes together with tools you probably have hanging around your garage.

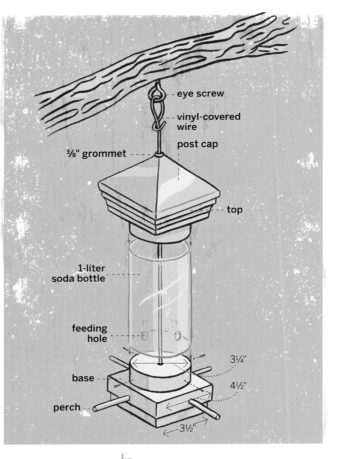

eye screw
vinyl-covered wire
post cap
⅜" grommet
top
1-liter soda bottle
feeding hole
base
perch
3¼"
4½"
3½"

ONLINE: Download the handy full-size templates for the top and base at thisoldhouse.com/books

STEP_1 Lay out and cut the parts

> Using a combination square and a compass, lay out the feeder's six individual pieces on a 2-foot-long cedar 1×6: three 3½-inch squares, one 4½-inch square, and two 3¼-inch-diameter circles.
> Clamp the cedar to a worktable. Using a jigsaw, cut out the circles and squares.
> Cut the four 4-inch-long perches from the ¼-inch dowel.
> Using a random-orbit sander or sanding block with 120-grit paper, sand the pieces so that they are smooth and free of splinters. (Make sure the dust bag is on the back of the sander.)

TO PARENTS: A jigsaw can send dust and splinters flying. Be sure everyone is wearing safety glasses before you cut.

STEP_2 Make the top

> Glue two 3½-inch blocks together, and secure them with 4d nails. Then glue and nail one of the circles on top of the blocks.
> Mix the epoxy, and spread it on one side of the square. Set the square into the copper post cap. Let it set for 20 minutes.

STEP_3 Build the base

> Turn the 4½-inch square on edge, and hold it steady with a bar clamp. Drill a ¼-inch hole about ½ inch deep into the center of the square's edge. Repeat until you have a hole on each edge.
> Glue 4-inch-long perches into the holes.
> Glue and nail the other circle onto the square with the perches.
> On the square side of the circle/square pair, drill a ¾-inch-deep hole into the center with a ½-inch spade bit. Exchange the spade bit for a ¼-inch bit, and drill all the way through the pair. The bigger hole will help hold the hanging wire in place.

48

HEY, KIDS! Here's a trick to find the center of the square: Just draw a diagonal line from each corner to the opposite corner to make an X on the face of the square. The place where the lines intersect is the center.

STEP_4 Wire the base

> Cut a piece of vinyl-covered wire about 3 feet long. Feed the wire through the hole in the base.
> Using a pair of pliers, fold over the wire's tip on the square side of the base to make a little knot. Pull the knotted end back into the larger hole until it stops at the circle. Make sure it's all the way in the hole and doesn't stick out of the square. Glue and nail the last 3½-inch square over the hole to cover it.

STEP_5 Make a hole for the wire in the top

> Put a bar clamp around the base of the post cap so that you can hold it steady. With a finish nail, make a little dent in the point of the copper peak. Then carefully drill a ¼-inch hole through the peak and out of the center of the attached circle.

STEP_6 Make the seed holder

> Using a pair of scissors, cut the ends off a 1-liter soda bottle to make a cylinder.

ONLINE VIDEO: Watch the step-by-step video at thisoldhouse.com /books

STEP_ 7
Assemble the feeder

> Brace the soda-bottle cylinder on a scrap of wood clamped to a worktable. Drill four evenly spaced ¼-inch holes 1½ inches from the cylinder's edge.

> Feed the wire attached to the base through the cylinder. Fit the cylinder over the circle on the base, positioning the feeding holes above the perches. Nail the cylinder to the base with blued tacks.

> Thread the wire through the top by going through the circle first, then out through the copper peak. Fit the top into the cylinder.

> To hold the top on, slide a rubber grommet onto the top of the wire, and push it tight against the copper peak. This is your assembled bird feeder.

50

STEP_ 8
Fill the feeder with seed

> Pull the grommet along the wire to loosen the top, pull the top out of the cylinder, then fill the cylinder with seed. Fit the top back on, pull the wire taut, and slide the rubber grommet tight against the peak again.

STEP_ 9 Make a hook for the feeder

> Choose a tree to hang your feeder from and a limb that's easy to reach. The limb should be healthy and thick enough to support the weight of a full feeder—plus a couple of birds.

> Twist an eye screw into the limb. Slide a screwdriver through the eye, and use it to turn the screw until it's in all the way.

STEP_ 10 Hang the feeder

> Thread the top end of the bird feeder's wire through the eye screw on the tree. Twist the wire around itself to keep it from slipping out. Then sit back and wait for your visitors to drop in for lunch!

WHAT BIRDS EAT

Fill your feeder with yummy treats to attract all kinds of birds. One sure bet: black-oil sunflower seed. The thin shells are easy to crack, and the seeds have lots of protein and fat. Here are some other foods that different birds like to eat.

BLACK-CAPPED CHICKADEE
Safflower seed, striped sunflower seed, sunflower hearts

← **ORIOLE**
oranges, apples, commercial mixed birdseed, cracked corn

52

↑ **SPARROW**
sunflower seed, commercial mixed birdseed

PAINTED BUNTING
safflower seed, suet, millet, peanut kernels

→ **ROBIN**
Sunflower hearts and chips, millet

BLUE JAY
Striped sunflower seed, sunflower hearts, peanuts, cracked corn

MOURNING DOVE
Safflower seed

← **CATBIRD**
suet, sunflower seed, nuts

↑ **CARDINAL**
Striped sunflower seed, sunflower hearts and chips, safflower seed, peanuts, millet

→ **JUNCO**
cracked corn, peanuts, nut meats

← **ROSE-BREASTED GROSBEAK**
sunflower seed, commercial mixed birdseed

build a sandbox

A SANDBOX brings a little bit of the beach into your backyard, and playtime is even more fun when the box itself has an imaginative shape. Kids can "drive" at the playground for hours of fun in this red car. It even has special storage under the hood for when you're ready to make a pit stop.

This project is a bit challenging, so older kids may want to help build it with the younger ones. You can construct the basic box in your garage, then park it on a level spot outside. With the whole family pitching in, it will take just one weekend to get this car roadworthy, so you'll soon be ready to roll.

$$$

COST>
$150–$200

TIME>
2 DAYS

DIFFICULTY>
There are many heavy parts, and the assembly is challenging.

TOOLS YOU'LL NEED>

- Tape measure
- Triangular layout square
- Jigsaw with coarse, wood-cutting blade
- 4-foot bar clamps
- Drill/driver with ⅛-inch bit
- Safety glasses
- Paintbrushes
- Compass
- Shovel and steel rake
- 4-foot level
- Utility scissors
- Staple gun

MATERIALS TO BUY>

- Four 8-foot pressure-treated 2×12s
- Two 8-foot pressure-treated ⁵⁄₄×6 decking boards
- One 6-foot pressure-treated 2×4
- 2 square feet of ½-inch pressure-treated plywood
- Steering-wheel cover
- 3-inch deck screws
- ¼×1-inch zinc fender washer
- Two drawer handles
- Two sets of 2½-inch stainless-steel butt hinges
- Latex exterior stain
- Latex exterior paint
- Landscape fabric
- 20 bags of play sand

{ HOW IT GOES TOGETHER }

The sandbox car has four sides and a seat all built from 2×12s. The ⁵⁄₄×6 decking forms the dashboard and the hood, which opens to reveal storage. Inside the box, landscape fabric lines the bottom and sides to keep weeds from growing up through the sand. The sand used to fill the box is a special debris-free, soft sand sold as "play sand."

The best way to build this box is to assemble it in a workspace, such as your garage, then move it to a level spot outside. Before you even cut the wood, you'll need to support the big pieces on blocks or sawhorses. And since the large 2×12s used for this project are so thick, you'll need to drill pilot holes anywhere you will be screwing parts together. You'll also need to clamp plywood pieces to a worktable before cutting them. Make sure the piece you're cutting off can fall freely.

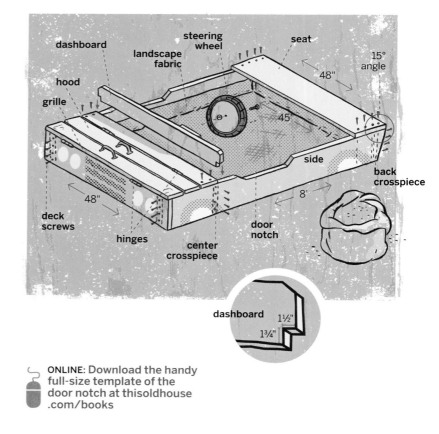

ONLINE: Download the handy full-size template of the door notch at thisoldhouse.com/books

STEP_1
Cut out the parts

> Cut one 2×12 into two 48-inch pieces for the grille and seat; cut another into two 45-inch pieces for the back and center crosspieces. Cut the decking into four 48-inch pieces for the hood and dashboard.

> Shape the tail fins by cutting off one end of each side piece at a 15-degree angle, making the end come to a point. Cut out the 1⅝-by-17¼-inch angled notches for the doors on each side.

> From the 2×4, cut four 11¼-inch corner supports and one 6-inch block for a steering wheel mount.

STEP_2
Line up the parts

> Drill four evenly spaced pilot holes into the back crosspiece, ¾ inch in from the ends. Then drill four evenly spaced pilot holes into the front grille piece, 2¼ inches in from the ends.

> Lay down each side piece, with the insides facing up, and attach the corner supports. The front corner supports should be flush with the front edge of the side; the back corner support is inset 1½ inches from the bottom edge of the tail fins.

> From the front end, measure 14¼ inches along each side. Drill four pilot holes down the face. This is where the center crosspiece will go.

STEP_3
Assemble the sandbox

> Stand the sides up again, and line up the back crosspiece between them. Screw through the pilot holes into the edges of the back corner supports.

> Line up the center crosspiece with its pilot holes, and fasten it in place.

> Put the grille across the front of the box, then screw it to the edges of the corner supports.

> Screw the seat to the top edges of the sides.

ONLINE VIDEO: Watch the step-by-step video at thisoldhouse .com/books

HEY, KIDS! You can help out by holding the pieces of wood together so that they don't wobble.

STEP_4
Add the dashboard

> Align the back edge of your first hood board with the back edge of the crosspiece. Screw the hood board onto the sides.

> Stand the notched dashboard up vertically, and line it up with the edge of the first hood board.

> Screw the dashboard to the back of the crosspiece.

STEP_5
Put on the hood

> Lay two hinges on the front edge of the first hood piece, about 8 inches in from the ends. Position them so that one leaf is on the decking and the other hangs over the front. Lay another piece of decking on top to hold the hinges in place.

> Screw the front leaves of the hinges to the edge of the first hood piece. Remove the top piece and stand up the hinges. Put the top piece back so that it is aligned with the first hood piece, and screw the other leaves onto its edge.

> Attach the second set of hinges to the grille, with the leaves hanging over the front. Flip the unattached leaves up, and screw them to the back face of the last hood piece. Now the hood doors will open in opposite directions.

STEP_6
Make the steering wheel

> Save the plastic or cardboard form the wheel cover came on, and use it as a template for the steering wheel.

> Place it on a piece of ½-inch plywood and trace around it.

> Clamp the plywood to the worktable. Using a jigsaw, cut out the steering wheel; you will have to stop in the middle of the cut to unclamp the plywood and turn it around so that you can finish.

TO PARENTS:
A jigsaw can send dust and splinters flying. Be sure you and your children wear safety glasses.

STEP_**7**
Paint it

> Stain the sandbox red, inside and out. Also stain the plywood steering wheel and the 6-inch block.
> Using a compass, draw wheels at the back end of the sides, with hubcaps inside them.
> Draw headlights and the grille pattern on the front of the sandbox.
> Paint the wheels and the grille pattern black, and the headlights and hubcaps silver.

STEP_**8**
Place the sandbox outside

> While the sandbox dries, find a level spot of ground for it. If necessary, dig out an area until it is level, then rake it smooth.
> Put the sandbox on the cleared spot of ground. Using a 4-foot level, check that the sandbox is level in both directions; if it isn't, rake or dig the ground underneath until it is.

STEP_ 9 Make the lining

> Unroll a piece of landscape fabric, and cut it long enough to fit along the bottom and up the sides of the sandbox. You will need two pieces to cover the width of the box.
> Line the bottom of the box with the fabric. Using a staple gun, attach the fabric a few inches up the sides. Tuck the fabric into the corners so that it won't rip when you add the sand.

STEP_ 10 Fill it with sand

> Fill the box with play sand. Using a metal rake, smooth the sand until it's level.

STEP_11
Affix the steering wheel

> Fit the wheel cover around the plywood steering wheel. Screw the 6-inch block to the dashboard where the steering wheel will go. Screw the wheel to the block through the center, using a washer between the two so that the wheel can spin.

STEP_12
Mount the hood ornament

> Attach the two handles to the hinged decking pieces so that they face each other to look like a hood ornament.

STEP_13
You're done!

> Grab your digging toys and hit the road!

BUILD A CASTLE

Sand castles aren't just for the beach. With your new slice of the shoreline right in your own backyard, you can build a sandy stronghold any time. Just study these basic parts, and you'll be able to custom design a perfect medieval fortress.

KEEP
This ultrafortified part of the castle is easy to mold from a milk carton with the top cut off.

BATTLEMENTS
These jagged wall toppers protect against attack; you can carve them out with a shovel or mold them with half an ice-cube tray.

PORTCULLIS
Make this gridlike gate out of Popsicle sticks or straws.

BARBICAN
Use shoe boxes or plastic food savers to build up the square walls of this outer defense.

GATEHOUSE
Put your carving skills to work forming the many sides and angles that make this defensive point so strong.

TOWERS
Empty cans and a funnel will make these strong, rounded wall connectors.

build an easel

ONE OF THE BEST WAYS to encourage your children's budding creativity is to give them a place to practice their talents. This sturdy, portable artist's easel is compact but holds colorful paints, brushes, pencils, markers, and more. And since it has two sides, your kids can enjoy drawing and painting with friends and siblings.

The frame is inexpensive to build, but the dry-erase boards can make the costs add up. To keep the price down, use ¼-inch plywood instead and cover it with chalkboard or magnetic paint.

Once you're done, set the easel up in the corner of a bedroom or playroom to create an artist's corner—and keep the mess all in one place. It's a perfect way for your little ones to discover their inner Picasso!

$$
COST> $125

TIME>
2 HOURS

DIFFICULTY>
It's easy to make, but cutting hardwood may slow things down.

{ HOW IT GOES TOGETHER }

The basic construction of this easel is simple: Hinged, square-cut boards make up the legs, while cross braces and side brackets hold it together. All the materials to make it can be found at a home center and a home goods or stationery store. But since the easel is made from a hardwood, parents will need to do the cutting and drilling. Kids can help out by measuring and marking the parts and, if they are comfortable holding a drill, by driving the screws into pilot holes.

TOOLS YOU'LL NEED>

- Tape measure
- Combination square
- Bar clamps
- Jigsaw
- Safety glasses
- Drill/driver with ³⁄₃₂-inch, ¼-inch, and ⅛-inch drill bits, and a 1¼-inch hole saw

MATERIALS TO BUY>

- Three 8-foot oak or maple 1×3s
- Two 23-by-23-inch magnetic dry-erase boards
- 1-inch dowel, 3 feet long
- Two 4-inch strap hinges
- 1¼-inch #8 wood screws and two washers
- Two plastic trays or kitchen drawer organizers
- ¾-inch #10 wood screws and eight washers
- One 2-foot-wide roll of paper

66

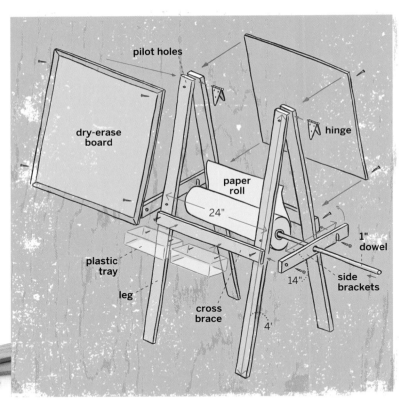

pilot holes

dry-erase board

hinge

paper roll

24"

1" dowel

plastic tray

14"

side brackets

leg

cross brace

4'

ONLINE: Download the handy full-size template for the side brackets at thisoldhouse.com/books

STEP_1
Lay out the pieces

> Using a tape measure, mark the midpoints (4 feet) of two 8-foot oak or maple 1×3s to make the four legs. Using a combination square, mark a cutline at each of these points.

> On a third 1×3, measure out and mark four shorter lengths: two 24-inch sections for the cross braces and two 14-inches sections for the side brackets.

HEY, KIDS! A combination square helps you make a straight line at a perfect right angle. Just hold the ruler part flat on the wood, and brace the square head against the edge while you mark your line.

STEP_2
Cut the wood

> Put on your safety glasses, and clamp a 1×3 to a worktable, making sure the cut mark hangs over the edge of the table. Using a jigsaw, carefully cut the pieces of the frame, stopping to move and reclamp the boards before each cut.

TO PARENTS: Sawing is best left to an adult, but kids can help out by catching the pieces as they fall. Just make sure they're standing far from the saw—and don't let them lift up on the wood as you cut, because that can pinch the blade.

STEP_3 Mark and drill the side brackets

> Each side bracket will pivot on a single screw and lock in place with a slot that slides over a second screw.

> Clamp a bracket to your worktable. Measure ¾ inch in from each end of the bracket, and, using a combination square, make lines at those points. Then find the middle of each line, and make a small cross mark. Make a third cross mark at the center of the whole bracket.

> Using a drill/driver fitted with a 3/32-inch bit, make a pilot hole at the center of the cross mark on one end of the bracket.

> At the other end of the bracket, extend the cross mark into a ¼-inch-wide slot that runs from the middle to the lower edge of the bracket. Using a drill/driver and a ¼-inch bit, make a hole at the cross mark at the top of the slot. Do this for both brackets.

STEP_4 Cut the slots

> Using a jigsaw, and with the bracket clamped to the worktable, cut along the slot lines to meet the ¼-inch hole. Repeat this process with the other bracket.

STEP_5
Drill the dowel holes

> Clamp the bracket to the table so that the cross mark in the center of the piece hangs over the edge. Using a drill/driver fitted with a 1¼-inch hole saw, make a large hole centered on the mark. This will fit the dowel that holds a roll of paper in the middle of the easel.

HEY, KIDS! The hole saw cuts out small plugs—don't throw them away. Paint them with your favorite designs, and glue a magnet on the back. Now you have decorative magnets for your easel.

STEP_6 Attach the hinges

> Line up two 4-foot legs end to end. Lay a strap hinge across the butted ends, allowing space for the hinge knuckles, and mark the wood at the hinge holes. Using a drill/driver fitted with a ⅛-inch bit, make pilot holes at your marks. Then attach the hinge by driving ¾-inch screws through the hinge holes and into the wood.
> Repeat for the other pair of legs.

STEP_7 Attach the cross braces and side brackets

> Lay down the two hinged sets of legs about 2 feet apart. Find the vertical midpoint of the legs at 24 inches. Line up one of the cross braces across the face of the legs so that the ends are flush with the outer edges of the legs and the top is at the midpoint mark. Drill one $\frac{3}{32}$-inch pilot hole at each end, through the cross brace and into the legs. For the best holding power, the holes should be diagonal. Attach the cross brace with 1¼-inch screws. Repeat with the other cross brace.

> Stand the easel up and open the legs wide enough so that the ends of the side brackets are flush with the ends of the cross braces. Mark the legs through the two holes in the bracket (the pilot hole and the slot hole). Using a $\frac{3}{32}$-inch bit, drill pilot holes into the legs at these marks.

> To attach the side brackets, slip a 1¼-inch screw through the pilot hole, then slide a washer over the shank at the back. Drive this screw into the leg, leaving it loose enough for the bracket to pivot.

> Drive another screw directly into the opposite leg; leave about ¾ inch of the screw sticking out. The slot on the bracket should slide over this screw.

ONLINE VIDEO: Watch the step-by-step video at thisoldhouse.com/books

STEP_8
Mount the boards

> Position a dry-erase board over the legs, its bottom aligned with the top of the cross brace. Using a ⅛-inch bit, drill pilot holes through the four corners of the board and into the legs. Attach the board through these holes using 1¼-inch screws.

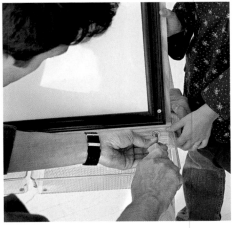

STEP_9 Put on the plastic trays

> Line up the plastic trays on the cross braces on the front and back of the easel, and mark the trays where you want to attach them. Lay the plastic trays on a piece of scrap wood and, using a ⅛-inch bit, drill through the marks on the plastic.
> Use the holes in the plastic to mark the cross braces for pilot holes, then drill them with a ⅛-inch bit. Attach the trays to the cross braces with ¾-inch screws fitted with washers.

STEP_10 Add the paper

> Slide the dowel through the hole in one side bracket, through the paper roll, and out the other side. Then pull the paper up through the opening in the top of the easel and down over one of the boards. Secure it with the magnets you made, and you're ready to paint and draw!

LEARN TO DRAW

Learning how to draw means learning how to see like an artist. To the artist's eye, a subject is composed of simple geometric shapes: the rectangle, the triangle, and the circle. Try the steps below to draw a few objects around the house. Before you know it, you'll be the artist in residence.

1 LEARN THE BASIC SHAPES

There are three basic shapes in drawing: the rectangle (and its little brother, the square), the triangle, and the circle. Practice drawing them a few times. Easy, right?

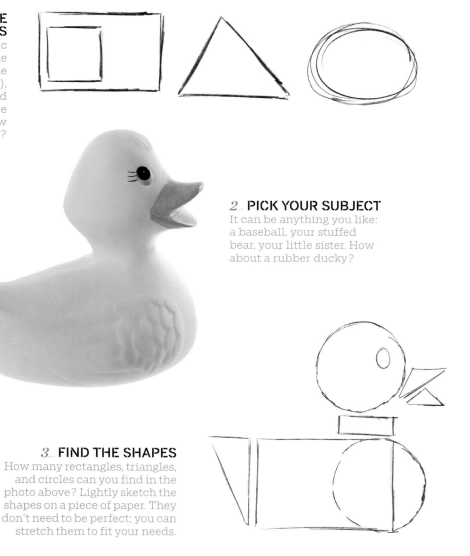

2 PICK YOUR SUBJECT

It can be anything you like: a baseball, your stuffed bear, your little sister. How about a rubber ducky?

3 FIND THE SHAPES

How many rectangles, triangles, and circles can you find in the photo above? Lightly sketch the shapes on a piece of paper. They don't need to be perfect; you can stretch them to fit your needs.

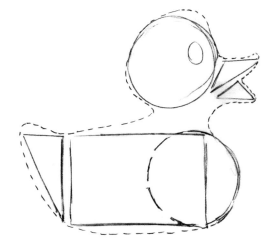

4. CREATE THE OUTLINE

Once you have your shapes, it's super easy to figure out the outline of the duck. His head is not completely circular—it peaks at the top. His tail is a little more rounded, as is his belly. Sketch the duck lightly at first until you are happy with the shape, then make the line heavier. Don't worry if you mess up; you can always erase it and start over.

5. ADD THE DETAILS

Now that you have drawn the main parts, how about some details? Look at the photo of the duck again. There are eyelashes to be added, short feathers on its chest, and long feathers at the tail. Now *that* looks like a duck!

EXTRA CREDIT

6. ADD SOME SHADING

For extra credit, add some shading to your drawing to give it more depth. Now you have a perfectly drawn rubber ducky!

build a lemonade stand

WHEN THE SUN IS HOT and kids are bored, there's nothing better to get them motivated than a project that comes with a built-in reward. This old-fashioned lemonade stand is sure to spark some creative interest, along with a bit of entrepreneurial spirit.

The stand is easy to assemble—slotted construction means no nails or screws—it's sturdy and colorful, and it comes apart quickly for storage. There's even a bonus: If kids need to display a science fair project or perform this week's puppet show, the table works just as well inside.

$
COST> $50

⏱
TIME>
3 HOURS

DIFFICULTY>
With its slotted construction, this project comes together quickly.

TOOLS
YOU'LL NEED>

- Tape measure and straightedge
- Combination square
- Spring clamps
- Drill/driver with ⅜-inch bit
- Jigsaw
- Random-orbit sander
- Paintbrush and roller
- Safety glasses

MATERIALS
TO BUY>

- 4-by-8-foot sheet of ½-inch birch veneer plywood
- Two 5-foot lengths of ¾-inch PVC pipe
- Two ¾-inch PVC end caps
- 120-grit sandpaper
- Latex primer
- Exterior latex paint
- Colored markers
- Card stock
- Velcro tape
- String
- Clothespins

{ HOW IT GOES TOGETHER }

This sturdy stand holds together the same way cardboard store displays do, with slots that fit into one another. The slots need to be just slightly longer than half the length of the smaller pieces so that all the edges are at an even height when the pieces are mated. The top of the stand has notches in the corners to fit around the interlocking sides. It helps to keep the whole assembly sturdy by bracing the pieces square to one another.

Parents should take on the job of sawing the slots and notches. But there's a lot to keep kids busy with this project: They can sand, paint, and make the sign. And once the table is all set up on a busy stretch of sidewalk, they can mix up a pitcher of ice-cold lemonade and prepare for the thirsty crowds to come running.

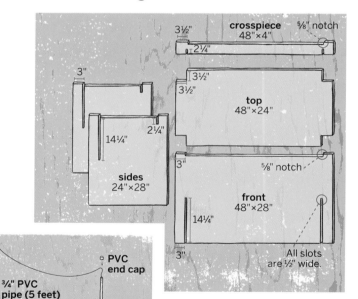

crosspiece
48"×4"
3½"   ⅝" notch
2¼"
3"   3½"
3½"
top
48"×24"

sides
24"×28"
14¼"   2¼"

3"   ⅝" notch
front
48"×28"
14¼"
3"   All slots are ½" wide.

¾" PVC pipe (5 feet)   PVC end cap

Velcro tape

ONLINE: Download the handy cutting guide at thisoldhouse.com /books

STEP_1
Lay out the parts

> Using a tape measure and straightedge, lay out the stand's five individual pieces on a 4-by-8-foot sheet of ½-inch birch veneer plywood: the front, two sides, the back-support crosspiece, and the top.

HEY, KIDS! You can help measure the parts so that your parents can cut them out!

STEP_2
Cut out the panels and notches

> Secure the plywood to the worktable with spring clamps before you cut. Using a jigsaw, cut out the five parts. With a combination square, lay out the corner notches on the top piece. Cut the notches with the jigsaw.
> Cut out the ⅝-inch notches on the crosspiece and the top of the front panel.

TO PARENTS: A jigsaw can send dust and splinters flying. Be sure everyone wears safety glasses.

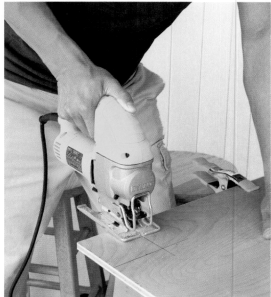

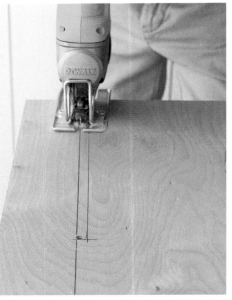

STEP_3 Cut the slots

> Using a straightedge and combination square, mark slots 3 inches in from the edges on the front, sides, and crosspiece—down from the top on the sides, up from the bottom on the front and crosspiece (see illustration, page 76). Make the long slots (on the sides and front) 14¼ inches deep and the short slots (on the crosspiece and sides) 2¼ inches deep.
> Using a drill/driver, make ⅜-inch holes inside the corners of the slots. Cut the slots with a jigsaw, using the holes to turn the blade.

78

STEP_4 Sand the wood

> Using a random-orbit sander and 120-grit sandpaper, sand down all the pieces so that they are free of splinters before you paint.

HEY, KIDS! You can help with sanding. Just make sure a parent watches you— or even holds onto the sander—because it moves a lot when it vibrates.

STEP_5 Paint the parts and make the sign

> Prime the wood with latex primer on all the sides and edges. Allow the primer to dry completely. Using exterior paint, finish the stand in your favorite colors. While the paint dries, make a sign by drawing the letters L-E-M-O-N-A-D-E on individual cards with colorful markers.

TO PARENTS: Speed the drying process by placing the pieces on sawhorses in the sun or setting up a drying station with fans in the garage.

STEP_6 Assemble the stand

>Stand up the sides, slots facing up. Slide the front, slots facing down, onto the sides. Then slide the crosspiece onto the back. Lay the top piece onto the stand, with the notches fitted around the interlocking side pieces.

TO PARENTS: Have kids hold the pieces steady while you put the slots together—and watch out for pinched fingers!

STEP_7 Attach the signposts

> Cut eight 1-inch tabs of Velcro tape. Keep both halves of the Velcro stuck together. Peel away one side of the paper backing and stick four tabs down each of the front corners of the stand. Peel off the other paper backing, and push a PVC pipe into each corner. Press hard so that the Velcro sticks to the pipe.

STEP_8 Hang the sign

> Cut a piece of string 1 foot longer than the distance between the pipes. Drop one end of the string 6 inches into the top of one pipe. Secure it with a pipe cap. Thread the other end of the string into the opposite pipe, and secure it the same way.
> Using clothespins, attach the sign cards to the string. Then get ready for thirsty customers!

ONLINE VIDEO: Watch the step-by-step video at thisoldhouse.com/books

JUICE RECIPES

You'll draw more thirsty customers if you offer them some flavorful choices. Here are a few different lemonade recipes, courtesy of Sunkist, to try out on the crowds that are sure to mob your stand on a hot day.

REAL OLD-FASHIONED LEMONADE

- 1 cup fresh-squeezed lemon juice
- 1 cup sugar, or to taste
- 4 cups cold water
  ice cubes
- 1 lemon, unpeeled, cut into cartwheel slices

In a large pitcher, combine the lemon juice and sugar; stir to dissolve the sugar. Add the remaining ingredients and blend well.

variations
PINK LEMONADE
Add a few drops of red food coloring or grenadine syrup.

HONEYED LEMONADE
Substitute honey to taste for the sugar.

MAKES 6 SERVINGS.

FRESH-FRUIT LEMONADE

- 1 cup fresh-squeezed lemon juice
- 1 cup sugar
- 1 cup ripe strawberries, sliced, or whole raspberries or blueberries
- 4 cups cold water
  ice cubes
- 1 lemon, unpeeled, cut into cartwheel slices

In a blender or food processor, combine the berries, lemon juice, and sugar; blend until smooth. Pour into a large pitcher. Add cold water, lemon cartwheel slices, and ice cubes; stir well. Garnish each serving with additional fruit or fresh mint leaves, if desired.

MAKES 6 SERVINGS.

TROPICAL LEMONADE

- 2 cups fresh-squeezed lemon juice
- 6 cups water
- 1 cup sugar
- 1 tablespoon ground ginger
- 16 1-inch pieces of fresh pineapple

Combine lemon juice, water, sugar, and ginger; blend well. Chill. Place ice cubes and four pineapple pieces in a tall glass and add chilled lemonade.

MAKES 4 SERVINGS.

PASSIONATE LEMONADE

- 1 cup fresh-squeezed lemon juice
- 3 cups water
- ½ cup sugar
- 4 cups passion-fruit-flavored tea (If the tea is presweetened, you may need to use less sugar.)
- 4 fresh lemon twists
  fresh mint sprigs

Combine lemon juice, water, and sugar; blend well to dissolve sugar. Add tea and mix well. Chill. Pour mix over ice cubes in glasses. Garnish with a lemon twist and mint sprig.

MAKES 4 SERVINGS.

This Old House
special project

build a mini-golf course

$$$
COST> $150

⏱
TIME>
3 HOURS

DIFFICULTY>
Easy to
moderate.
The layout is
straightforward.

MINI-GOLF IS A GREAT GAME for bringing together family members of every age. Who doesn't love besting Dad on the loop-de-loop hole? But it doesn't have to be just a vacation-week treat. Wouldn't it be great to have your very own course to play all year round—inside or out?

This Old House TV's plumbing and heating expert, Richard Trethewey, and general contractor, Tom Silva, designed a great course that you and your family can build in an afternoon. It is made up of panels that you can take apart and rearrange to make the game as easy or hard as you like. Create as many panels as you need for 1, 2, or even 18 holes. Then give everyone a putter, and they'll have a ball—literally—trying to navigate the obstacles you set for them.

Richard Trethewey
TOH TV Plumbing & Heating Expert

TOOLS
YOU'LL NEED>

- Miter box with backsaw
- Drill/driver with 4-inch and 2¾-inch hole saws
- Spring clamps
- Plastic drop cloth
- Framing square
- Utility knife
- Hacksaw

MATERIALS
TO BUY*>

- One 2×4-foot sheet of ¾-inch medium-density fiberboard (MDF)
- Five deck balusters
- Wood glue
- Cyanoacrylate glue (aka Krazy Glue)
- 1½ yards of 72-inch-wide green felt
- Spray adhesive
- 3-inch PVC pipe fitting (coupling, cap, or adapter)
- Five composite wood balusters (such as Trex)
- Outdoor welcome mat or artificial turf
- Two 5-gallon buckets
- Duct tape
- Three 2-inch PVC elbows
- Flexible plastic sign

* Materials list is for a single panel. The course shown is made up of four panels.

{ HOW IT GOES TOGETHER }

Rich, Tom, and their crew of young builders made this mini-golf course from medium-density fiberboard (MDF), a stable wood composite material. It's smooth and easy to work with, and it makes a great flat surface for rolling a golf ball. You can find MDF in several standard sizes at the home center, so you won't need to cut it up if you design your course with these sizes in mind.

Rich and Tom covered the course with green felt and lined the golf holes with PVC pipe fittings. They came up with two great obstacles—a loop-de-loop and a ramp with redirects—to challenge even the best putters. You can add tunnels, water hazards, and ramps to your course, or just use your imagination to create different ways to enjoy hours of entertainment with your golf game.

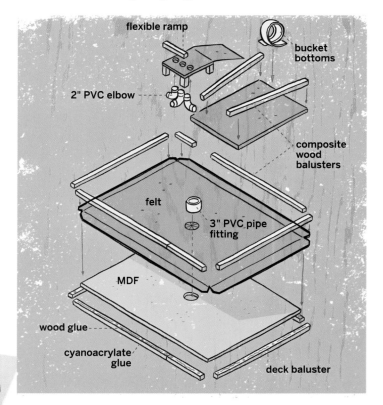

flexible ramp

bucket bottoms

2" PVC elbow

composite wood balusters

felt

3" PVC pipe fitting

MDF

wood glue

cyanoacrylate glue

deck baluster

STEP_1 Lay out and cut the baluster supports

> Line up the deck balusters along the edges of a sheet of MDF. Mark them to fit around the entire sheet, corner to corner and flush with the edges.
> Using a miter box and backsaw, cut the balusters to length.

TOM SILVA SAYS:
"Using a miter box is a great way for kids to learn how to saw properly. It controls their movements and teaches them to let the saw do the work."

STEP_2 Glue the baluster supports in place

> Line up the balusters next to the edges of the MDF. Squeeze several strips of wood glue onto each baluster, one baluster at a time. Leave a few inches of space between the strips of wood glue. In the spaces, put down dabs of fast-setting cyanoacrylate glue.
> If you are using two-part cyanoacrylate glue, spray it with activator. Quickly turn over the baluster onto the MDF, line it up, and hold it in place while the cyanoacrylate sets. This glue acts as a clamp while the wood glue dries into a strong bond.

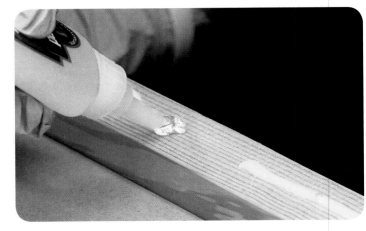

This Old House special project

STEP_3 Cut the hole

> Measure across the MDF panel, and mark it slightly off-center, closer to one end. Using a drill/driver fitted with a 4-inch hole saw, start making a hole at this mark. Once the bit has poked through, flip the panel over and finish the cut from the other side. This will keep the MDF from splintering.

86

STEP_4 Stick the felt to the panel

> Place a 54-by-72-inch piece of felt on a worktable. Stretch it slightly, and hold it in place with spring clamps. Place the MDF on a plastic drop cloth, away from the felt.
> Spray the top of the MDF with adhesive. Work in long, even strokes across the whole board. Spray the felt with adhesive as well. Let both pieces dry according to the instructions on the can.
> Check the felt to make sure it's perfectly smooth. Turn the MDF over and hold it over the felt, being careful not to let the two touch. Place the panel on the center of the felt, and press it down.
> Spray more adhesive around the hole and on the balusters on the bottom of the panel. Let it dry.

Cut the felt corners

> Using a framing square and utility knife, cut away the excess felt at each corner. Hold the square corner to corner with the panel, and cut 1½ inches in each direction. At those points, cut away the felt diagonally.

Wrap the sides

> Get some helpers to lend a hand. Have them pull evenly along all sides of the felt, then lift and wrap the felt over the balusters.

Wrap the hole

> Cut the felt in the hole into sections like a pizza. Pull up each wedge and wrap it tightly to cover the sides of the hole.

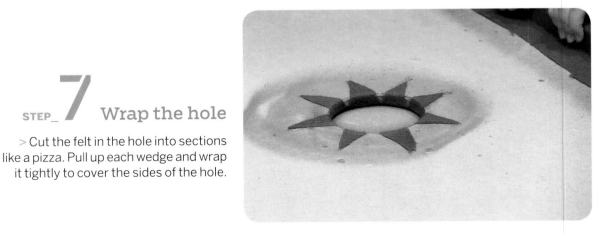

This Old House special project

STEP_8
Finish the hole

> Using a hacksaw, cut the PVC pipe fitting into a piece about 2 inches tall. Turn the panel over, and drop the fitting into the hole.

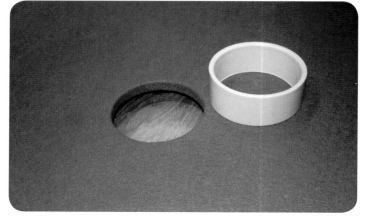

STEP_9
Line the course

> Line your course with lengths of composite baluster. These are heavy enough to stay in place, and balls bounce nicely off them. You can also adjust them to customize your holes.
> Add short, angled pieces to create corner bumpers.

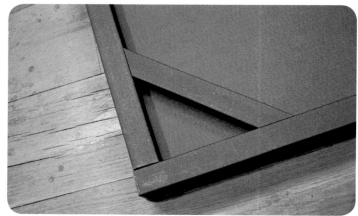

STEP_10
Make the rough

> Cut islands out of a green welcome mat or artificial turf to form the rough. Place these patches around the course to create obstacles for your players.

ONLINE VIDEO: Watch the step-by-step video at thisoldhouse.com/books

STEP_**11**
Make a loop-de-loop

> Cut the lower 3 inches off two 5-gallon buckets. Cut out the buckets' bottoms, leaving a 1-inch band. Then cut an opening through each circular piece.
> Marry the pieces to form a channel. Line up the open ends, and spread them apart to create a loop. Once the loop is adjusted, secure it with duct tape, and screw the sides to a block made of two short, angled pieces of composite baluster.

STEP_**12**
Make a flexible ramp

> Using a drill/driver fitted with a 2¾-inch hole saw, cut a row of three holes in the center of a 12-inch square of MDF. Flip the MDF over, and glue 3¼-inch composite legs at each corner, creating a platform.
> Build the ramp by taping a flexible plastic sign to the edge of the platform. Wrap the top of the platform and the ramp in green felt, and cut out the three holes.
> Insert the elbow fittings into the bottom of the platform, twisting them in different directions. Add a bumper of composite baluster to the top of the platform.
> Now you're ready for some mini-golf. Grab your putter and hit the links!

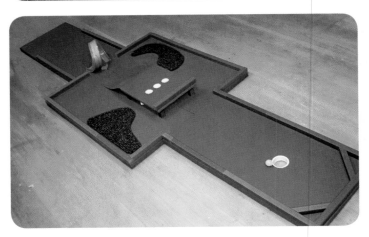

project>

build a toy chest

OPEN UP A TOY CHEST and a child's imagination takes flight, especially if the chest itself is part of the fun. This toy chest looks like a barn, designed to make even a city dweller feel a little bit country. A bonus: With wheels on the bottom and special toy box lid supports, it's easier than ever for kids to round up their toys when playtime is over.

You can make this chest in an afternoon with tools on hand and materials available at the home center. Kids can handle most of the work that includes measuring, nailing, sanding, and painting, while adults should do the sawing and clamping. Once the toy chest is put together, kids will be scrambling to fill it with their prized possessions.

$$
COST> $95

TIME>
5 HOURS

DIFFICULTY>
Fitting the parts together takes a little extra patience.

{ HOW IT GOES TOGETHER }

The toy chest is made from birch veneer plywood, with four sides that fit around a rectangular bottom. The roof fits over the two triangular gables at the ends. It's easiest to build the roof by first clamping the gables to the box, then attaching the front and back roof pieces in place. That way you're sure to end up with a lid that fits the box perfectly, with a pleasing overhang on the front edge that makes it easy to flip open.

For sturdiness, the roof is attached to the bottom box with a long continuous hinge all the way across one edge. To accommodate the hinge, the back of the box and the roof are both slightly shorter than the corresponding front pieces, and the back ends of the gables are clipped off slightly. For safety, there are also two toy box spring lid supports, which hold the weight of the roof and close softly with a gentle push of your child's hands. These keep the box from slamming on little fingers. Casters attached to the bottom of the chest make it easier to move around for play and cleanup.

TOOLS YOU'LL NEED>
- Tape measure
- Combination square
- Straightedge
- C-clamps
- Safety glasses
- Jigsaw
- Random-orbit sander
- 36-inch bar clamp
- Hammer and nailset
- Drill/driver with ⅜-inch bit
- Putty knife
- Small paint rollers and brush
- Hand screwdriver

MATERIALS TO BUY>
- 4-by-4-foot piece of ½-inch birch veneer plywood
- 120-grit sandpaper
- Stainable wood glue
- Rag
- 4d finish nails
- Stainable wood putty
- Four 2-inch casters
- Satin-finish latex paint in red, white, and silver
- Painter's tape
- 30-inch continuous hinge
- Two toy box spring lid supports (one left and one right)

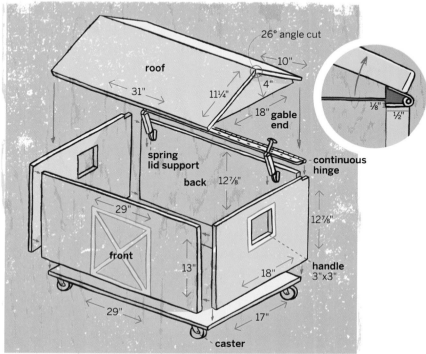

roof
26° angle cut
10"
31"
11¼"
4"
18" gable end
⅛"
½"
spring lid support
continuous hinge
back
12⅞"
29"
12⅞"
front
13"
18"
handle 3"x3"
29"
17"
caster

STEP_1 Lay out and cut the parts

> Using a tape measure and straightedge, lay out the chest's nine individual pieces on a half sheet of ½-inch birch veneer plywood: front, back, two sides, bottom, two roof sections, and two gable ends, using the measurements in the illustration.

> Clamp the plywood to a worktable. Using a jigsaw, cut the front, back, two sides, and the bottom pieces.
> To make the roof pieces, set the saw blade at a 26-degree angle. Cut along one long edge of each roof piece at that angle; when mated together, these cuts will form the angle of the peak. Cut all the other edges with the blade set straight at 0 degrees.
> On each side piece, mark out a 3-by-3-inch square for the handle. Drill ⅜-inch holes inside the four corners of each square to fit a jigsaw blade. Using a jigsaw, cut out both squares. Also cut a ⅛-by-½-inch notch on the top back corners.
> Cut each gable out of a 4-by-18-inch piece of plywood. Clip ½ inch off the back corner to match the notch in the side pieces.

93

STEP_2 Sand the pieces

> Clamp the pieces to the worktable and use a random-orbit sander with 120-grit sandpaper to smooth the wood until it's free of splinters. Make sure to hold onto the sander tightly because it can spin away from you.

ONLINE VIDEO:
Watch the step-
by-step video at
thisoldhouse
.com/books

STEP_3 Glue the pieces

> Run a thin bead of wood glue along all edges of the bottom piece. Apply glue to the side edges of the front and back and to the corresponding faces of the side pieces. Stand them up around the bottom piece. Let the sides overlap the front and back, and make sure the notched corners line up with the back piece.

STEP_4 Clamp the box

> Hold the box together with bar clamps. Use a damp rag to wipe up any glue that squeezes out.

STEP_5 Nail the box together

> Nail along all the edges—sides as well as bottom—with 4d finish nails every 3 to 4 inches. Using a nailset, sink all the nails below the surface. Fill the holes with wood putty.

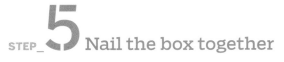

STEP_6 Build the roof

> Stand the triangular gable ends on edge with the cut-off corners to the back, and clamp them in place on top of each side of the bottom box. Use pieces of scrap wood to bridge the seam, and brace them so that they stay vertical. Be sure not to glue or nail these gable ends down—they are meant to be the forms on which the roof is built, and assembling the pieces in place on the box will ensure that the roof ends up straight.

> Glue and nail the shorter roof section onto the gable ends, aligning it so that the angled edge is centered over the peak of the gables and the back edge is even with the back of the box. It should be perfectly centered at the top but overhang the cut-off corner of each gable by about ½ inch.

> Position the front of the roof to meet up with the back so that the angled edges form a tight peak. The front of the roof should overhang the front of the box.

STEP_7 Nail the roof together

> Glue and nail the front section of the roof onto the gable ends, making sure the whole roof assembly looks centered, with a ½-inch overhang on the gable ends.

> Set all the nails below the surface, and fill the holes with wood putty.

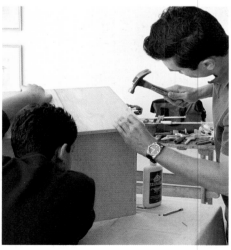

STEP_8
Paint the toy chest

> Once the wood putty is dry, sand it smooth with 120-grit sandpaper. Turn the box over and mount the casters to the four corners.
> Using rollers and brushes, paint the barn roof silver and the base red. Let it dry.
> Mark off the front door, corners, and frames around the handles with painter's tape, then paint them white.

STEP_9 Attach the roof with hinges

> Line up the continuous hinge on the top back edge of the box. Make small divots at each screw hole along the back of the box with a nail.
> Using a drill/driver, screw the continuous hinge to the box. Then screw the hinge to the roof.
> Attach the right and left lid supports according to the manufacturer's instructions.
> Now fill your toy chest with your favorite toys!

BUILD SOME TOYS

Now that your kids have the coolest toy chest around, why not make some toys to go inside it? If you feel comfortable with a jigsaw—or better yet, if you have a scroll saw—you can easily cut up the scraps left over from the toy chest to make these simple items.

OLD-FASHIONED PULL TOY
Cut out your favorite animal shape, and attach wooden toy wheels (you can find some at rockler.com). Tie on a string and you've got a toy that will keep a toddler busy for hours.

SPINNING TOP
You don't need a lathe to turn a top—just cut out some circles of different sizes and glue them together to make the top shape. Screw on a wood bead for a handle, hammer a blunt nail through the last circle, then twirl away.

JIGSAW PUZZLE
Take apart your favorite picture, then put it back together for loads of fun. Print out an image—maybe a beach, a horse, or your family portrait—and use mounting spray to glue it to a piece of plywood. Cut it into interlocking shapes, then challenge the family to reassemble it.

build a soccer goal

WHETHER YOU HAVE a budding athlete in your household or you just want to get everyone to play as a family, having a soccer goal in the backyard is a win-win. The goal shown here has a basic design and is easy to build, so it can be assembled in an afternoon. And chances are good that you have the home field advantage, with the right tools already on hand and the materials easy to get at the home center. Because it's made from PVC pipes and deer netting, this goal is so lightweight and easy to move that you can set it up whenever you're ready to play. Just put it out to turn the backyard into a playing field, and you'll be ready to score!

$$
COST> $55

TIME>
2 HOURS

DIFFICULTY>
There are many parts, but they're a cinch to cut and fit together.

{ HOW IT GOES TOGETHER }

The goal shown here is a three-dimensional triangle made from PVC plumbing pipes wrapped in deer netting. And while the instructions are for a 4-by-5-foot goal, you can adapt the measurements to make your goal any size you want. The best part is that cutting and assembling the sections of pipe are so simple and safe, kids can help out at every step. They'll be amazed at how quickly they can cut through the plastic pipes, and they'll have a ball assembling the 22 different PVC pieces like a giant puzzle. Just be sure a parent supervises the gluing stage, as the short time you have to adjust the pipes before the glue sets means working quickly. Deer netting, a strong but supple mesh, is an inexpensive alternative to a rope net, and it attaches easily to the pipes with common zip ties.

TOOLS
YOU'LL NEED>
- Tape measure
- Hacksaw
- Utility scissors
- Permanent marker

MATERIALS
TO BUY>
- Four 10-foot lengths of 1¼-inch PVC tubing
- Six 1¼-inch PVC elbows
- Four 1¼-inch PVC tees
- 80-grit sandpaper
- PVC pipe cement (preferably a low-VOC formula that's labeled all-weather)
- Deer netting
- Five dozen zip ties
- Small sand bags (optional: to hold down the goal when you play)

100

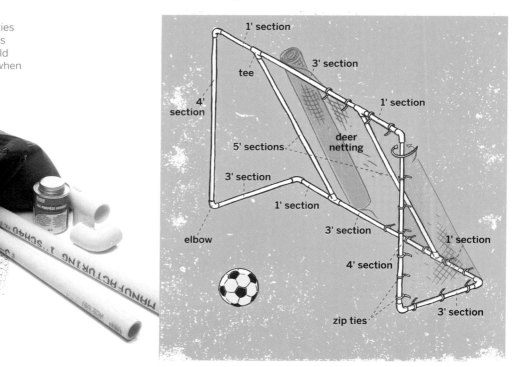

ONLINE: Download a diagram for the best way to divide the pipes at thisoldhouse.com/books

STEP_1
Lay out the pieces

> Using a tape measure, divide the four 10-foot lengths of PVC pipe into the sections needed to assemble the frame of the goal, and mark one section of each length for cutting. You will need two 5-foot sections, two 4-foot sections, four 3-foot sections, and four 1-foot sections.

HEY, KIDS! Try out your hacksaw skills. Start with a slow, small stroke on your cut mark to make a little groove. Then, once your blade gains purchase, use long, straight strokes to cut all the way through the pipe.

STEP_2 Cut the pipe

> Lay a marked-up pipe on a worktable, with your first cut mark hanging off the edge. Cut the pipe at the mark with a hacksaw. Use your first cut piece as a guide for the others—that way they'll all be the same length. Continue until all the pieces are cut. You should be left with one unused 6-foot piece.

> Using 80-grit sandpaper, smooth out the cut ends of the pipes so that there are no sharp edges or burrs.

STEP_ 3
Dry-fit the frame

> Before you apply the glue and assemble the goal permanently, you will need to dry-fit the pieces together. This will ensure that the sections of pipe fit together correctly and the goal is straight and true.

> Begin with the base. Make the two corners by attaching a 1-foot section to a 3-foot section, using an elbow. Lay these down facing each other. Put tees on the other ends of the 1-foot sections. Then connect the two tees with a 3-foot section.

> To make the top of the goal, repeat the steps above, except attach the 1-foot sections to 4-foot sections at the elbows.

> Attach elbows to the short sides of the base, and turn them so that they face upward. Stand the top of the goal up, and insert the bottom of the 4-foot sections into the elbows. You should now have an L-shaped frame.

> Finally, connect the top and base tees with 5-foot sections that act as brace pieces.

TO PARENTS: Use the side of the goal to teach older kids about right triangles and the Pythagorean theorem: $a^2 + b^2 = c^2$. The base side is a (3 feet), the vertical side is b (4 feet), and the brace piece is the hypotenuse, or c (5 feet).

STEP_ 4
Keep track of the connections

> Using a permanent marker, draw a line across the adjoining parts at every connection. This will help you line up the pipes once you glue them and put the goal back together perfectly before the PVC cement has a chance to dry.

STEP_5
Glue the frame together

> Take apart one of the joints. Wipe PVC pipe cement on the outside of the pipe and the inside of the connector, then fit the two back together. Quickly line up your marks and hold the fittings in place. Pipe cement sets in seconds, so you don't have much time.
> Continue to take apart each joint, apply the pipe cement, and put it back together in this manner until the entire frame is glued up.

STEP_6 Make the net

> Take the soccer goal outside. Unroll the deer netting and measure out enough to cover the back and sides of the goal. Using utility scissors, cut the netting to size, leaving a little extra for overhang.

ONLINE VIDEO: Watch the step-by-step video at thisoldhouse.com/books

STEP_ **7** Attach the net

> Wrap the netting around the goal posts, leaving it a little loose so that it catches a soccer ball without tearing. Then feed zip ties through the netting and around the pipes, connecting the ties and pulling them tight. Do this every few inches until all the netting is attached. Using utility scissors, snip off the long ends of the ties, and turn the joints to the back so that they're hard to see.

HEY, KIDS! Your little hands can be a big help when it comes to threading the ties through the netting. Just be sure to have a parent check that they're connected tightly.

STEP_ **8** Cut off the excess netting

> Using utility scissors, trim off the excess netting around the front and bottom of the goal.
> If you like, you can use small sandbags or stakes in the corners of the goal to hold it down. Then grab some players, start a game, and see how long it takes to score your first goal!

COOL SOCCER MOVES!

Now that you have the soccer goal, you need to learn important soccer footwork. Here are some of the basic maneuvers you can use to get your ball past the other team.

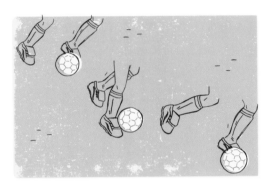

DRIBBLING

This is essential to the game—it's how you move the ball without using your hands. Tap the ball between your feet as you run down the field—aim for the laces of your sneakers. Try it without looking down, if you can, so that you can see where you're going and watch for the other team.

STEP OVER

Fake out your opponent with this move. Step to the ball as if you are going to kick it in one direction, but step over it instead. Quickly plant your other foot down for support, and—bam!—kick the ball away with the outside of your foot. Off you go!

INSIDE CUT

This basic soccer move allows you to quickly change directions so that you can stay one step ahead of your opponent. Dribble the ball in one direction, then cut in front of the ball with one foot. You will momentarily stop the ball, but it will be protected between your feet. Then move it in the opposite direction and accelerate away!

This Old House special project

build a raised garden

HERE'S A GREAT PROJECT for the budding gardener in your family. *This Old House* TV landscape contractor Roger Cook recently built a raised garden with a few young friends. It's a simple frame of rot-resistant lumber that holds soil in place and brings it to a height that's easy for everyone to reach without stepping onto precious plants—plus no more dirty knees (or at least fewer dirty knees).

Plant a vegetable patch in your new garden. Kids will have tons of fun caring for their seedlings as they mature. And what better reward is there for a garden well tended than a crisp carrot straight from the earth (washed, of course) or a nice ripe tomato right from the vine.

$$$
COST> $225

TIME>
2 HOURS

DIFFICULTY>
Simple, but an adult should run the power saw and fill the bed with soil.

Roger Cook
TOH TV Landscape Contractor

TOOLS
YOU'LL NEED>
- Jigsaw or circular saw
- Drill/driver
- Framing square
- Edger or spade
- Sod cutter or grub hoe
- Pitchfork or rotary tiller
- 4-foot level
- Sledgehammer
- Wheelbarrow
- Reciprocating saw or handsaw

MATERIALS
TO BUY>
- One 8-foot length of 2×10 cedar
- Two 10-foot lengths of 2×10 cedar
- Two 10-foot lengths of 2×4 cedar
- 3-inch deck screws
- Garden soil
- Compost
- Starter fertilizer appropriate for vegetables
- Vegetable seeds or seedlings
- Grass clippings for mulch

{ HOW IT GOES TOGETHER }

Roger and the kids made this bed with rot-resistant cedar, a material that's safe around the edible plants it will contain. Cedar will also turn a nice silvery gray as it weathers.

The bed here is 10 feet long, but you can make yours as long as the lumber allows. However, it should be no more than 4 feet wide so that little arms can reach the plants in the middle. Roger cut stakes from 2×4s and angled one end to a point to hold the frame in place and keep the sides from bowing once it's filled with heavy soil.

Vegetable gardens need a lot of light, so Roger and his helpers placed the bed in an area that gets sun for most of the day. To improve drainage and prevent weeds from growing up into the garden, he removed the grass beneath the bed and tilled the earth before adding soil.

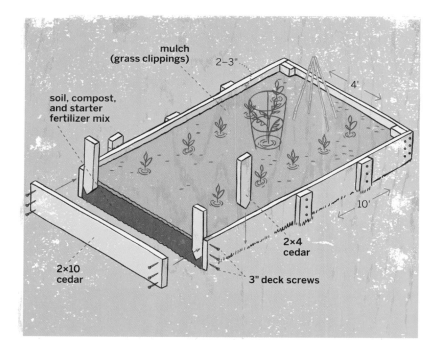

mulch (grass clippings)

2–3"

4'

soil, compost, and starter fertilizer mix

2×4 cedar

10'

2×10 cedar

3" deck screws

ONLINE VIDEO: Watch the step-by-step video at thisoldhouse.com/books

STEP_1 Cut and assemble the frame

> Using a jigsaw or circular saw, cut an 8-foot length of 2×10 cedar in half.

> Hold one of the 10-foot 2×10s on edge, and butt the end of a 4-foot 2×10 up to it so that the face of the longer board overlaps the end of the shorter board. Using the drill/driver, sink three 3-inch screws through the face of the long side and into the end of the short side.

> Attach the other sides together, using three 3-inch screws on each corner and overlapping the long sides over the short sides.

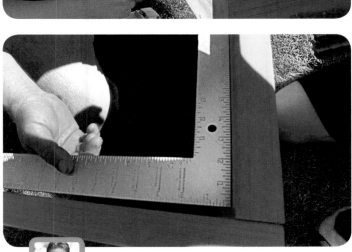

STEP_2 Square up the frame

> With the four sides assembled, place a framing square in each corner, one at a time, and adjust the frame until the corner lines up square. After aligning the entire frame, check all four corners again with the framing square.

ROGER COOK SAYS: "The great thing about a raised garden is that you can put in the perfect soil for whatever you want to grow."

This Old **House**
special project

STEP_**3**

Brace the corners

> Leaving the corners perfectly square, tack scrap lumber across each one with 3-inch screws to hold it in position.

STEP_**4**

Mark the perimeter

> Move the frame to the sunny spot you've picked out for the bed. Using an edger or spade, mark the ground around the perimeter of the frame.

STEP_**5**

Prepare the soil

> Set the frame aside. Using a sod cutter or grub hoe, skim away the grass layer. Increase drainage for your garden by turning the soil beneath the bed area with a pitchfork or rotary tiller.

STEP_ 6 Level and stake the frame

> Set the frame back in place over the tilled area. Using a 4-foot level, check the position of the frame. Dig out the soil beneath the frame until it sits level on all sides.

> Cut ten 2-foot-long pieces of 2×4. Make two diagonal cuts on one end of each piece to create a point. Using a sledgehammer, drive these stakes at least 18 inches into the ground along the outside of the long sides of the frame at 2½-foot intervals. Using the drill/driver, secure each stake to the frame with three 3-inch screws.

> Remove the temporary corner braces. Drive a stake inside each corner. On one short side of the bed, secure the stakes with screws driven through the frame on both sides of each corner. On the other short side, leave the screws off.

STEP_ 7 Fill the bed

> Remove the unscrewed short side of the bed. Using a wheelbarrow, fill the bed with a mixture of soil and compost. Level out the soil and continue filling until it is 2 to 3 inches from the top of the frame.

This Old **House**
special project

STEP_ **8**
Reassemble the frame

> Replace the short side of the bed and, using a drill/driver, secure it to the long sides and to the corner stakes with 3-inch screws. Using a reciprocating saw or handsaw, cut the top of each stake flush with the top of the frame.

STEP_ **9**
Plant the vegetables

> Plant seeds or seedlings for your vegetables. Dig a small hole for each one, mix in the appropriate amount of starter fertilizer, set the seed or seedling into the hole, then cover it with soil.
> Once the bed is planted, water it thoroughly. Then cover the soil with about an inch of mulch made from grass clippings.

ROGER COOK SAYS:
"Use grass clippings to mulch around the plants. This will help keep the soil moist and stop weeds from growing."

TEND YOUR GARDEN

Children gravitate to gardening for very basic reasons: Dirt. Water. Hole digging. They also love to watch seeds sprout, leaf out, and eventually bear flowers or tempting tomatoes. Here are some tips on how to keep their veggie garden green.

AIM FOR FAST GRATIFICATION

If you're going to start seeds indoors, you can create a perfect nursery using the bottom of a cardboard egg container and a starter soil mix. Or use peat pots—the compressed ones that expand with water like those magic sponges are a fun bonus.

Go for plants that germinate quickly, like radishes—even if you don't like to eat them. They mature in three or four weeks. If you begin in early spring, you'll have to acclimate the seedlings to the outdoors for a few hours a day before you plant them. When they're ready, just cut the egg carton containers apart to separate the plants. Like peat pots, the little cardboard forms can go right in the ground, where they will decompose as the plants grow.

If seeds are too slow for eager new farmers, buy small nursery plants to give your garden a head start. Some easy-to-grow vegetables are summer squash, peas, cucumbers, carrots, and tomatoes. Equally easy flowers include marigolds, nasturtium, ageratum, bachelor's buttons, cosmos, alyssum, and zinnias. You can try herbs like lavender and basil, too.

This Old **House** special project

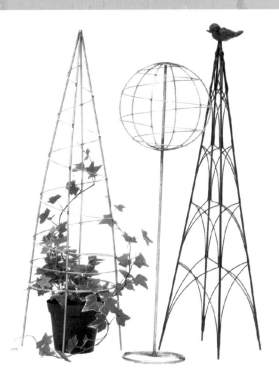

PROTECT THE YOUNG ONES

Shelter delicate plants and help retain moisture and heat in early spring with a glass cloche. You can also use it to warm the soil before you plant if you're starting your garden early in the spring. Make your own cloche with an empty drink container by cutting off the bottom.

TRY RACING FOR THE SKY

Peas, pole beans, and many squash-family plants, including cucumbers, gourds, and melons, will readily climb a support structure if you provide one. It saves space and reduces insect damage and rot by keeping the edible parts off the ground. You can screw (or even glue) a yardstick to a garden stake and use it to track a vine's progress, just like your kid's growth chart. Make it a race, and plant several different plants in a row, each with its own marker. School-age kids may want to keep a garden journal to record their planting project's progress.

MAKE WATERING FUN

There are no fixed rules on how much you should water. The easiest way to check the soil is to stick a finger in it down to the first knuckle; if it's dry, water the bed. Another idea is to install a rain gauge in your garden. Kids will have fun monitoring how much rainwater accumulates. Water your plants if there is less than 1 inch of water in the gauge per week during summer.

EMBRACE THE EXTREMES

Kids like small-fry fare that fits their fingers just as much as the giant and the wacky produce that'll wow their friends. You can find seeds for unique vegetables and fruits such as the ones shown here at your local garden center or online at websites like burpee.com or parkseed.com. Just plant them, then watch these small wonders grow.

Carrot Kaleidoscope
These crunchy carrots come in four great colors.

Watermelon Everglade Hybrid
Try this seedless melon, which looks like a bowling ball.

Red Lightning Tomatoes
Streaked with yellow, these tomatoes are a tangy treat.

Big Mama Lima Beans
Plant your very own magic beanstalk.

Romanesco Veronica
This Italian delicacy looks like a lime-green seashell.

Carrot Nandrin Hybrid
Win a county fair ribbon with these giant carrots.

Pepper Red Popper
These tiny peppers are perfect snacks straight from the garden.

build wall cubbies

$

COST> $25

⏱

TIME>
2 HOURS

DIFFICULTY>
Both the cutting
and assembly
are simple, and
the finishing is
very basic.

IT'S A SURE SIGN of independence when older kids want to have a say in how their bedroom is decorated. An easy way to satisfy that need is by making these modular wall cubbies, which can be customized to suit children's changing tastes as they grow. You can make just one cubby or stack several to create more space for a kid's imagination and creativity.

The cubbies shown here are 12-inch cubes, but you can make them any size you like. Even if you make them wider or taller, the construction is the same. For extra fun, the fabric-covered panels inside are removable, so you can change a cubby's look as often as kids change their mind.

TOOLS YOU'LL NEED>

- Tape measure
- Straightedge ruler
- Jigsaw, circular saw, or handsaw
- Bar clamps
- Safety glasses
- Random-orbit sander or sanding block
- Hammer and nailset
- Putty knife
- 2-inch paintbrush
- Small artist's brush
- Drill/driver with 1⁄16-inch bit
- Staple gun

MATERIALS TO BUY>

- One quarter-sheet of 1⁄2-inch birch veneer plywood
- One quarter-sheet of lauan or 1⁄4-inch plywood
- Stainable wood glue
- 4d finish nails
- 1-inch box nails
- Stainable wood putty
- 120-grit sandpaper
- Clear acrylic finish or latex paint
- Acrylic artist's paint
- 2-inch screws with corresponding washers and wall anchors
- 1⁄2 yard of fabric
- 1⁄4-inch staples
- Velcro tape

{ HOW IT GOES TOGETHER }

To make a cube out of 1⁄2-inch plywood, you need to cut the sides 1 inch shorter than the top and bottom pieces that overlap them. The thickness of the two pieces adds 1 inch, evening out the dimensions of the four sides. Similarly, the lauan or plywood piece that covers the back has the same dimensions as the box, but the piece that fits inside is 1 inch smaller in both width and height. (To get a head start on the cutting, ask a home center or lumberyard to rip the plywood into 12-inch-wide strips when you buy it.)

As with any wood project, the strongest way to hold things together is with both glue and nails. The glue multiplies the strength of the nails. Kids can do the nailing with some supervision; in fact, they can do most of the work, including measuring, sanding, stapling, and painting. A jigsaw is better off in adult hands, but kids as young as 7 should be able to use a random-orbit sander with a parent's guidance. And remember: Whenever the saw is on, safety goggles are a must.

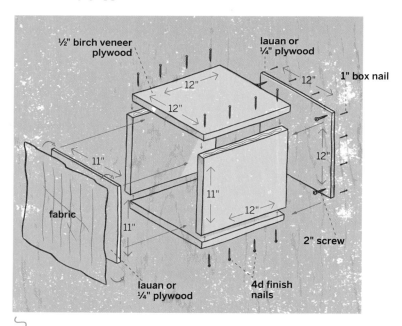

ONLINE: Download the handy full-size template at thisoldhouse.com/books

STEP_1 Lay out and cut the parts

> Using a tape measure and straightedge, mark up some birch veneer plywood to make the two 12-by-12-inch top and bottom pieces and the two 11-by-12-inch sides. Also, mark up some lauan to make one piece that's 12 by 12 inches and one that's 11 by 11 inches. Clamp the plywood tightly to a worktable. Then, using a jigsaw (a handsaw or circular saw will also work), cut the four sides.

TO PARENTS: Here's a chance to do a stealth math problem with your kids. Ask them why the two sides have to be shorter than the other parts to make a perfect cube.

STEP_2 Glue up the boards

> Run a thin bead of wood glue along the 12-inch edges of the 11-by-12-inch boards. Then make a box by overlapping the ends with the 12-by-12-inch boards. Hold the glued box together with bar clamps.

STEP_3 Nail the box together

> Secure the sides by nailing 4d finish nails every few inches along the edges of the top and bottom. You'll need about four nails on each side.
> Remove the clamps.

HEY, KIDS! Practice your nailing skills. Hold the hammer toward the end of the handle. Keep your eye on the nailhead while tapping firmly. And don't worry if you mess up—you can always take the nail out and try again!

STEP_4 Put on the back

> Lay a thin bead of wood glue around the entire back edge of the box. Then lay the 12-by-12-inch piece of lauan over it. Nail it in place using 1-inch box nails around the perimeter.

STEP_5 Fill and sand the box

> Using a hammer and nailset, sink all the finish nails on the sides just below the surface of the wood. Then, using a putty knife, fill the holes with putty. Let the putty dry, and wait a few minutes for the glue to set as well.
> Using a random-orbit sander with 120-grit sandpaper, smooth the plywood sides of the cubby to prepare them for finish. Kids can help with sanding—just make sure a parent watches, because the sander moves a lot when it vibrates.

STEP_6 Paint on the finish

> Using a 2-inch brush, coat the top, bottom, and sides of the cubby with a clear acrylic coating (for a wood finish) or latex paint (for a colored finish). Let it dry, sand it lightly, then apply a second coat. To add a colorful touch, use a small brush and acrylic artist's paint to match the front edge of the box to the fabric that will decorate the inside panel. Let it dry completely.

ONLINE VIDEO: Watch the step-by-step video at thisoldhouse.com/books

TO PARENTS: Make sure you use the right kind of anchors for your wall: plastic ribbed anchors for plaster and screw-in anchors or toggle bolts for drywall. If you hit the wall framing, that's even better—screw directly into that and skip the anchor altogether.

STEP_7 Secure the boxes to the wall

> If you want to stack up more than one box, you'll need to secure them to the wall so that they can't topple over. Hold the box where you want it to sit and, using a drill/driver fitted with a ¹⁄₁₆-inch bit, make a small hole through each of the four corners of the back panel and into the wall.

> If you did not hit the wall framing, you will need to properly anchor the holes.

> Reposition the box over the holes. Use a screwdriver to mount the box with 2-inch screws fitted with washers and driven through the lauan and into the wall framing or anchors.

STEP_8 Make the panel insert

> Cut a 13-by-13-inch square of the fabric. Lay it facedown, then put the 11-by-11-inch piece of lauan in the center. Fold one edge of fabric onto the lauan and, using a staple gun with ¼-inch staples, tack it at the middle. Fold the opposite side over, and pull it tight before stapling it. Continue to staple the fabric on by working your way out from the middle and alternating sides. Do the same for the other two sides until the fabric is smooth and covers the lauan.

HEY, KIDS! Staple guns are great for attaching fabric to wood, but you need to make sure the head is flat on the workpiece—and never pointed at anyone—before you squeeze the handle.

122

STEP_9 Put in the back panel

> Cut four small tabs of stick-on Velcro tape. Keep both halves of the Velcro stuck together. Peel away one side of the paper backing, and stick a tab onto each of the four corners of the back of the decorative panel. Peel away the paper backing on the other half of the Velcro tape while it's still on the decorative panel.
> Push the panel into the box and press hard. Wait a few minutes before pulling the panel back out; it should leave behind the other half of the tape, which will allow you to change the panel whenever you want to give your cubbies a different look. With the panel in place, start filling the cubbies with your favorite things!

STYLE YOUR CUBBY

Fabric-covered lauan is one way to add color to your cubbies, and it's easy to switch it out when you want a new decor. But you don't need to limit yourself to textiles to give your boxes a personalized touch. To change the look of your units, try some of these ideas:

CORK BULLETIN BOARD

Keep track of postcards or important to-do items on a miniature bulletin board. Just cut a cork tile to an 11-by-11-inch square, and use it instead of the inside panel of lauan. Add pushpins, and you're ready to go!

MAPS

Go around the world without leaving your room. Find a map of the United States or a country you want to visit, and staple it to the lauan.

PLEXIGLAS PHOTO DISPLAY

If you've got special pictures of family and friends, why not frame them in your cubby? Glue your photos to a piece of 11-by-11-inch construction paper, and cover them with an 11-by-11-inch piece of Plexiglas.

build a bat house

BATS ARE UNDERRATED. Besides being the only mammal that flies, most North American bats are nocturnal insectivores, which means they feed on night-flying insects—especially mosquitoes. In fact, a small bat can devour more than 600 mosquitoes in a single hour. They also eat beetles, wasps, and moths. So encouraging bats to nest near your house is a natural way to keep your yard bug-free.

This bat house is easy to make in an afternoon. Its shallow construction is designed specifically to attract bats, which like cramped, dark spaces for nesting. Kids can do lots of the work involved in making this bat house, including measuring, driving screws, and painting. Parents need to help out with the sawing. Once you've finished it, hang your bat house high in a sunny corner of your backyard, and the bats will soon find a stylish new home.

$$

COST> $60

TIME>
4 HOURS

DIFFICULTY>
The assembly is pretty easy, but cutting the bat shape might be a challenge.

TOOLS
YOU'LL NEED>

- Tape measure
- Combination square
- Straightedge
- Spring clamps
- Safety glasses
- Jigsaw
- French curve and circle templates
- Drill/driver with ¼-inch bit
- Caulk gun
- Staple gun

MATERIALS
TO BUY>

- 2-by-4-foot section of ½-inch exterior-grade plywood (not treated)
- One 6-foot 1×2
- ½-inch deer netting
- Exterior latex paint (black and another color)
- Low-VOC adhesive caulk
- 1-inch deck screws
- ⅜-inch staples
- 3½-inch deck screws

{ HOW IT GOES TOGETHER }

Bats are very particular about where they'll live, and their houses have to be constructed in a specific way that encourages them to nest. The inside of this house is painted black to keep it dark and warm, and the outside is a color that makes it blend in with the surroundings. The space where they go inside the house and roost is only about ¾ inch thick (with a small gap for air circulation). Still, dozens of bats will be able to live in this box and raise their pups.

When working on this project, keep safety in mind at all times. A jigsaw is better off in adult hands, but kids can help out by caulking, driving screws, attaching the netting, and painting. Make sure everyone has safety glasses on when the saw is in use, and keep sleeves away from power tools.

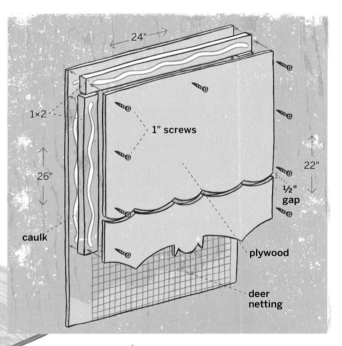

 ONLINE: Download the handy full-size template of the bat cutout at thisoldhouse.com/books

STEP_1 Measure and cut the plywood

> Using a tape measure and straightedge, mark up for cutting a 2-by-4-foot piece of ½-inch exterior-grade plywood: You'll need one piece that's 2 feet wide and 26 inches long and one that's 2 feet wide and 22 inches long. Clamp the plywood to a worktable. Make sure you have on safety glasses, then use a jigsaw or a circular saw to cut the plywood.

HEY, KIDS! French curves are great for helping you draw the bat wings, but you can also trace cans or cups to make curves of different sizes.

STEP_2 Draw the bat design

> Print out the template for the bat cutout. Or create your own bat shape using circular and oblong templates called French curves (available at most office supply stores). Lay out the bat shape on the edge of the shorter piece of plywood—just make sure it's 24 inches wide.

STEP_3 Drill holes for the jigsaw

> Clamp the plywood with the bat design to your worktable, making sure the whole bat hangs over the edge. Using a drill/driver with a ¼-inch bit, drill holes just inside the points of the bat shape. This will make it easy to turn your jigsaw blade as you cut out the curved parts.

STEP_4 Cut out the bat

> Using a jigsaw fitted with a narrow scroll blade, which is designed for making intricate curves, cut out the bat design. Cut the shape closest to the edge first, then cut the whole bat from the sheet. Because both halves of the cutline need to look clean, work slowly and carefully. Whenever you get to a drill hole at one of the points, stop the saw and turn it before you continue.

128

STEP_5 Make the sides

> To raise the front panel off the back and create a small crawl space to house the bats, you'll need strips of lumber around the edges. Cut three pieces from a 1×2: one 24-inch piece and two 19-inch pieces.

STEP_6 Attach the sides

> Using a caulk gun, lay a bead of caulk along the face of the long 1×2. Line it up with the top edge of the larger piece of plywood, and clamp it in place with spring clamps. Using a drill/driver, drive 1-inch deck screws through the 1×2 and into the plywood every 6 inches to hold it in place.

> Attach the two shorter pieces to the sides in the same manner, and caulk the ends where they meet the top piece before you clamp them down. Use a damp rag to wipe up any caulk that oozes out.

HEY, KIDS! You can help out with the caulking while your parents get the clamps ready.

STEP_7 Paint the parts

> Using a brush and roller, paint the back piece black, from the top edge to the ends of the 1×2s. Also paint the back of the front piece black. These will form the dark inside of the bat house.

> Paint the other surfaces in a color that will help maintain a healthy temperature inside the house. If you live in the North, a dark color can keep the house toasty by absorbing the sunlight. In the warm South, a light color may be a better choice. (See the map on page 133 for the best shades for your location.) Be sure all surfaces of the wood are painted and well sealed. Let the paint dry completely.

STEP_8 Attach the netting

> Unroll the deer netting, and lay it over the inside of the back section, flat against the plywood. Using a staple gun, attach the netting to the inner edge of the top 1×2 and along the sides. Make sure to pull it taut so that it can't sag when bats hang from it. Extend the netting all the way over the bottom edge, and wrap it around to the back. Once it's stapled all around, cut off the excess.

STEP_9 Attach the front piece

> Caulk along the face of the 1×2s on the back section. Place the front piece onto the 1×2s, with the bat shape facing the bottom, and the top edges and corners lined up. Clamp it in place. Drive 1-inch screws every 6 inches through the face and into the 1×2s to secure it.

STEP_10
Put on the bat cutout

> Caulk the exposed sections of the 1×2s, then place the cutout onto them, just below the large front piece. Leave a ½-inch gap between the two for the air vent. Clamp the piece, and attach it in place with a single 1-inch screw on each side.

ONLINE VIDEO: Watch the step-by-step video at thisoldhouse.com/books

STEP_11 Hang it up!

> Hang your bat house under the eaves of your house or from a tall, flat pole made from pressure-treated lumber. (Make sure to bury one-third of the lumber in the ground to keep it steady.) Attach it by driving 3½-inch deck screws through the corners into the siding or fascia of your house or, if you're using a pole, along the middle at the top and bottom.

> The bat house should be at least 15 feet off the ground, away from bright lights. Choose a place that faces south so that it gets plenty of sunlight (aim for 6 to 10 hours of exposure). This will keep it nice and hot—just the way bats like it!

BATS! BATS! BATS!

Did you know that there are more than a thousand bat species worldwide? Amazingly, bats make up almost a quarter of all mammal species on earth. You may already have bats around your house and not know it. Here are five species common to North America so that if you build a bat house, you'll know who's moving in.

HEY, KIDS! Did you know that bats have been around since dinosaurs roamed the earth?

132

↑ BIG BROWN BAT

The big brown bat has fur that is shiny brown and wing membranes, ears, feet, and face that are dark brown to blackish in color. It navigates as it flies by using ultrasonic sound waves and listening to the echo to locate objects, a process known as echolocation. This bat is a nocturnal insectivore, eating many night-flying insects, such as beetles and wasps.

LITTLE BROWN BAT →

As its name implies, this species looks like a smaller version of the big brown bat but with a pointy nose. It likes to eat wasps, beetles, and gnats—and it particularly loves mosquitoes, which is why it often roosts near water.

↓ EVENING BAT

This insect-eating bat is mostly brown or gray, with added spots of red, orange, or yellow fur. Some even have white patches or stripes. Evening bats grow up fast: Pups can fly within three weeks of birth.

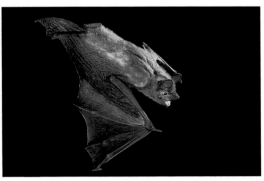

↑ PALLID BAT

Its eyes are bigger than most other species of North American bat, and it has pale, long, wide ears. It likes to eat crickets and can consume up to half its weight in insects every night.

← MEXICAN FREE-TAILED BAT

This medium-size dark brown or gray bat is one of the most abundant mammals in North America. It has wide-set ears that help it use echolocation to find its prey. This insectivore likes to roost in large numbers and is very important to insect control.

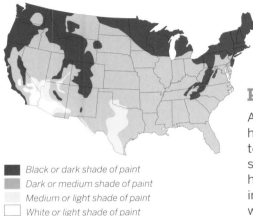

- ■ Black or dark shade of paint
- ■ Dark or medium shade of paint
- ■ Medium or light shade of paint
- □ White or light shade of paint

Source: Bat Conservation International

Pick your bat house color

According to Bat Conservation International, bats like their houses painted. Paint or stain helps maintain the sunlit temperature of the house, which is important to the day-sleeping bat. The darker the exterior color, the more heat the house will absorb from the sun, which may be a toasty treat in Maine, but rather stifling in Arizona. This map shows you what color ranges might work in your region.

build a tree swing

ALL KIDS WANT TO FLY, and every time they ride on a swing they get closer to that Peter Pan moment. But you don't need a whole playground to feel the spring breezes swoosh by. All you need is a seat, a rope, and a sturdy tree.

Making this swing requires few tools, and all the hardware needed to hang it can be found at your local home center. The seat is inexpensive—you can even make it out of scrap wood. Quality hardware and rope increase the cost but are important for safe swinging. In one morning you can put the parts together, get the rope in place, and start your magic ride!

$$$

COST> $135

🕐

TIME>
3 HOURS

DIFFICULTY>
Cutting
hardwood can
be tricky, and an
adult should
hang the swing.

{ HOW IT GOES TOGETHER }

This swing is made from a single hardwood board and comes together quickly. Two pieces cut from a 1×8 board form one broad, 14½-inch-wide seat. A third piece, glued and screwed across the seam of the seat, supports it from underneath.

The whole assembly hangs from one rope tied around a tear-shaped metal holder called a thimble. The thimble keeps the rope from fraying as it swings on a carabiner, or spring clip, hooked through an eyebolt, which is threaded through a strong tree limb.

It's important that the limb the eyebolt goes through is at least 8 inches thick and very healthy so that there is no chance it will break under the weight of a child swinging. It also has to be big enough to hold the bolt several feet from the tree trunk, to keep the seat swinging freely.

TOOLS YOU'LL NEED>
- Tape measure
- Combination square
- Bar clamps
- Jigsaw
- Drill/driver with ³⁄₁₆-inch drill bit, 1-inch spade bit, and long ⅝-inch spade bit
- Compass
- Random-orbit sander
- 2-inch paintbrush
- Small artist's paintbrush
- Screwdriver
- Wrench

MATERIALS TO BUY>
- 1×8 oak, maple, or other hardwood board, 4 feet long
- ¾-inch polypropylene rope
- 120-grit sandpaper
- Exterior-grade wood glue
- 1¼-inch deck screws
- Exterior latex paint
- Carabiner or spring clip
- ⅝-inch-thick, 10-inch-long stainless-steel or galvanized eyebolt with washer and two nuts
- ¾-inch rope thimble

ONLINE: Download the handy full-size template at thisoldhouse.com/books

136

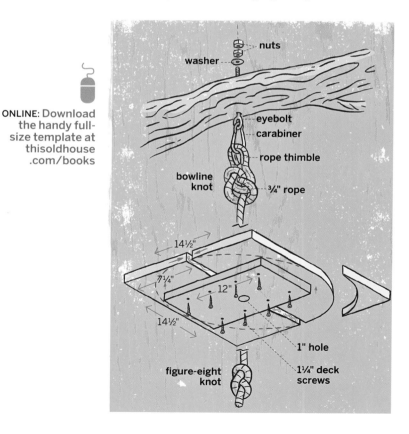

nuts
washer
eyebolt
carabiner
rope thimble
bowline knot
¾" rope
14½"
7¼"
12"
14½"
1" hole
figure-eight knot
1¼" deck screws

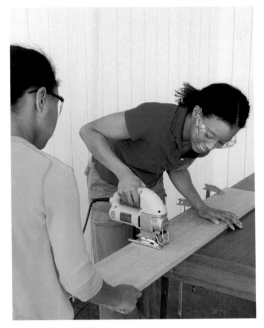

STEP_1 Lay out and cut the parts

> Using a tape measure and a combination square, measure out the three pieces of the swing on the 1×8 board: two 14½-inch-long sections for the seat and one 12-inch-long support brace that goes underneath.
> Clamp the wood tightly to a worktable. Using a jigsaw, cut the three pieces from the board.

TO PARENTS: A jigsaw can send dust and splinters flying. Be sure you and your children wear safety glasses. The helper should be sure to catch the wood, not lift it, so that the saw blade is not pinched.

STEP_2 Glue the seat together

> Run a thin bead of wood glue on the long edge of one 14½-inch wood piece. Fit it side by side to the other 14½-inch piece, then clamp them together tightly with bar clamps. This is your seat.
> Allow the glue to dry.

STEP_3 Attach the seat support, and drill the hole for the rope

> Glue the 12-inch support board across the seam in the middle of the seat bottom, with the long edges of the board perpendicular to the seam. Clamp the pieces together. Drill eight pilot holes through the support with a ³⁄₁₆-inch bit. Each long side of

the support should have four evenly spaced holes, two on each side of the seam. Attach it to the seat with 1¼-inch screws.

> Flip the seat so that it's faceup. Draw two diagonal lines from corner to corner, making an X. As if cutting a pie, draw another X over it, for eight equal slices. Put the point of a compass at the center, then draw the largest circle that will fit on the seat.

> Clamp the seat to the worktable. Using a drill/driver fitted with a 1-inch spade bit, drill a hole for the rope at the center of the seat.

HEY, KIDS! This is a great way to learn about circles, squares, and diameters.

STEP_4 Cut out the seat

> Using a jigsaw, cut out the seat shape. Halfway through the cut, you'll need to unclamp the seat, turn it around, and clamp it again before you finish making the whole circle.

> If you want your seat to look like a flower, like this one, make a mark ½ inch on either side of each radiating line along the circle's edge. Then mark each line ½ inch from the edge. Using a jigsaw, cut between these points to shape the curved edges of the petals.

> Using a random-orbit sander, smooth away splinters, and round over any sharp edges.

STEP_5
Paint the design

> Using exterior latex paint, brush the background color onto the seat. Coat the entire surface—top, bottom, and edges—to seal the wood. Allow the paint to dry.
> Draw the flower or other pattern in pencil on the background color. Use artist's brushes to fill in the design with more exterior paint.

STEP_6
Drill through the tree limb

> Pick out a tree with a healthy limb that's parallel to the ground and at least 8 inches thick. Make sure there's room for the seat to swing freely without hitting the tree trunk.
> Using a long ⅝-inch spade bit, drill a hole vertically through the center of the limb.

TO PARENTS: Be sure the tree limb you choose is alive and healthy so that it won't break under a child's weight.

STEP_7
Attach the eyebolt

> Thread an eyebolt through the hole so that the eye faces down. Slip on a washer, then two nuts, one after the other. Use a wrench to tighten the two nuts as you hold the loop of the bolt steady with a screwdriver.

ONLINE VIDEO: Watch the step-by-step video at thisoldhouse .com/books

STEP_8 Hang the swing with rope

> Tie one end of a long rope into a bowline knot around a thimble. Connect the thimble to the eyebolt with a carabiner. Slip the dangling end of the rope through the hole in the seat. Tie a figure-eight knot under the seat so that it sits at a comfortable height for the kids. Now you're ready to fly!

HEY, KIDS! What are some other knots you can tie a rope into?

PAINT YOUR SEAT

A circular seat is a great canvas for lots of different patterns and designs. Here are some other ways to decorate your swing.

TARGET
Make believe you're an Olympic archer.

SMILEY FACE
Smile and swing all day long.

FLYING SAUCER
Head into space on an adventure.

BASKETBALL
If you like to shoot hoops, this is the seat for you.

CLOCK FACE
Tell time using your legs as the clock's hands.

STOP SIGN
Pretend you're an officer of the law.

SUN
Spread a little sunshine in your backyard.

STAR
Make believe you're a shooting star.

STEERING WHEEL
Pretend you're driving a sports car.

BASEBALL
Pitch a no-hitter in your backyard.

thank you

We hope these projects were fun for you, because they sure were for us. We were lucky to work with some very talented people on this book. It all started with the design ideas of Edward Potokar and the crew of *Ask This Old House.* Edward, Tom Silva, Richard Trethewey, and Roger Cook came up with some truly imaginative projects for your family to enjoy. Alexandra Bandon, our online editor and a diligent taskmaster, produced the step-by-step instructions. She did a terrific job.

The photos and illustrations in this book are the products of Wendell T. Webber, a wonderful photographer, and Carl Wiens, a gifted illustrator. Wendell remained unflappable when faced with our hectic schedule. He shot literally thousands of photos and, despite all that, continues to work for us (thank you). Carl created a series of illustrations that are as fun as they are informative—no easy feat. Their wood-grain charm actually inspired the design of this book (just check out the facing page).

We'd also like to thank the families and kids who participated in the projects. They endured long days without complaint and added a genuine warmth to these pages.

And finally, we would like to thank many of the hardworking folks at *This Old House:* Scott Omelianuk, Amy Rosenfeld, Denise Sfraga, Yoshiko Taniguchi-Canada, Douglas Adams, Allison Chin, Robert Hardin, Cynthia Ng, Carolyn Blackmar, Timothy E. Pitt, Jennifer DeMeritt, Michael Svirsky, and Al Rufino.

ISBN-10: 0-8487-3395-9
ISBN-13: 978-0-8487-3395-7
Library of Congress Control Number:
2009941792

Printed in the United States of America
First Printing 2010

Oxmoor House

VP, Publishing Director: **Jim Childs**
Editorial Director: **Susan Payne Dobbs**
Managing Editor: **Laurie Herr**
Brand Manager: **Fonda Hitchcock**

This Old House Ventures Inc.

President: **John L. Brown**
Editor, This Old House: **Scott Omelianuk**
Publisher: **Charles R. Kammerer**

TOH Fun Family Projects

Editor/Art Director: **Hylah Hill**
Technical Editor: **Mark Powers**
Project Designers: **Edward Potokar,
Tom Silva, Richard Trethewey, Roger Cook**
Project Producer: **Alexandra Bandon**
Design Director: **Amy Rosenfeld**
Photo Editor: **Denise Sfraga**
Principal Photographer: **Wendell T. Webber**
Principal Illustrator: **Carl Wiens**
Editorial Operations Director: **Carolyn Blackmar**
Editorial Production Manager:
Yoshiko Taniguchi-Canada
Copy Editor: **Jennifer DeMeritt**
Proofreader: **Timothy E. Pitt**
Prepress Coordinator: **Al Rufino**
Design and Prepress Manager: **Ann-Michelle Gallero**
Book Production Manager: **Susan Chodakiewicz**

Credits

To order additional publications,
call 1-800-765-6400 or 1-800-491-0551.

For more books to enrich your life,
visit **oxmoorhouse.com**

To search for more DIY projects and
home ideas, visit **thisoldhouse.com**

For more exciting garden and
home ideas, visit **myhomeideas.com**